ALL THE SEASONS OF MERCY

ALL THE SEASONS OF MERCY

Diane Karay

The Westminster Press
Philadelphia

Book design by Christine Schueler

First edition

Published by The Westminster Press®
Philadelphia, Pennsylvania

PRINTED IN THE UNITED STATES OF AMERICA
9 8 7 6 5 4 3 2

Library of Congress Cataloging-in-Publication Data

Karay, Diane, 1954–
   All the seasons of mercy.

   Includes indexes.
   1. Church year—Prayer-books and devotions—English.
I. Title.
BV30.K33 1987   264'.13   86-18948
ISBN 0–664–24067–4 (pbk.)

For my parents,
Alexander and Luella Karay

"But God hath made no decree to distinguish the seasons of his mercies. . . . In heaven it is alwaies Autumne, his mercies are ever in their maturity. . . .

"God comes to thee, not as in the dawning of the day, not as in the bud of the spring, but as the Sun at noon to illustrate all shadowes, as the sheaves in harvest, to fill all penuries, all occasions invite his mercies, and all times are his seasons."
                                                                    —*John Donne (1624)*

"Speak gentle words—for fallen on the knives
These sentient hearts and these exceeded lives
Bleed till their pitying Advocate arrives."
                                                —*Amos Niven Wilder (1972)*

CONTENTS

PREFACE

All the Seasons of Mercy is a book of prayers intended primarily for congregational worship, but it is also suitable for private devotional reading. Its unifying theme is expressed in John Donne's idea that all times are God's seasons, all occasions invite God's mercy. The prayers are grouped according to the seasons of the church year. They draw on the seasons of the calendar year as one source of imagery. Worship leaders living in non-temperate climates should feel free to adapt them for local use.

These prayers were written to enrich the worship of a small Presbyterian church. To me the prayers were gifts of God. I hope that they will be a gift to those who pray them, leading women, men, and children to a richer sense of conversation with God.

All scripture adaptations are from the Revised Standard Version. In addition, all scripture references are to the prescribed reading or readings from the Common Lectionary (1982) unless enclosed by parentheses.

It has not been the intention to provide a complete series of prayers for the three-year lectionary cycle. On the one hand, the indexes will show at a glance where to find those prayers which are related to specific scriptures, days, seasons, and years. On the other hand, many prayers can be used, or adapted for use, on Sundays other than those for which they were written, and without reference to the scriptures on which they are based. For example, a prayer based on the lectionary readings for a given Sunday in Year C can be used, with slight adaptation, on any Sunday in Year A if it is deemed appropriate for the season, or has the desired emphasis.

All prayers in sections titled "Prayers of Confession or Affirmation" are prayers of confession, unless designated as prayers of affirmation in the information following the prayer.

Prayers of intercession and the Lord's Prayer may follow all pastoral prayers. The intercession allows prayer for individuals' concerns as well as contemporary social, national, or international concerns, which would date quickly if included in the body of the pastoral prayer.

Those who wish to coordinate these prayers with the Common Lectionary readings will recall that the current cycle is as follows: Advent through Pentecost 1986–87 (Year A); 1987–88 (Year B); 1988–89 (Year C).

In this book, the numbers of the Sundays after Pentecost, and the readings assigned to them, have been synchronized with the liturgical calendar through the 1988–89 church year. In subsequent years there will be some variation. The surest way to find prayers and responsive readings related to Pentecost lections is to consult a current liturgical calendar and the Index of Scriptural References.

Pentecost Prayer of Praise 17 and Pentecost Unison Prayer 19 were previously published in *Concern,* December 1984 and February 1986, respectively.

I wish to thank the following people who helped me with the book: the congregation of The Presbyterian Church, Rantoul, Illinois, with whom these prayers were prayed; Ann Page-El for encouragement at a crucial and fortuitous time; James G. Kirk, who saw a latent book in a simple file of prayers, and who by his encouragement, support, and assistance helped bring this book to birth; my friends Karen Davis-Brown and Steven Shoemaker for their patience, affirmation, and editorial help; Perry LeFevre for suggestions on theological content; William Bodamer and the Religion Department of Millikin University for a fellowship allowing concentrated work on the manuscript. In addition I owe a debt of gratitude to the late Marion Overholser, my fifth grade teacher, who crowned my first literary effort with the prediction that I would someday write a book. I am very grateful to my husband, Joseph K. Nose, for editorial help, for his support and love, and for his faith in the creative Spirit that moves me to write.

DIANE KARAY

8th Sunday After Pentecost, 1986

ADVENT
AND CHRISTMAS

CALLS TO WORSHIP

1.

LEADER: As quietly as the winter steals upon us, the season of joy approaches.

PEOPLE: We wait for our Redeemer, for God's promise to be fulfilled.

LEADER: The day is coming quickly. The God of mercy draws near.

PEOPLE: Therefore we wait with joy, attentive to all the signs of his coming.

ALL: Come quickly, Lord Jesus!

> 1st Advent, Year C
> Jeremiah 33:14–16
> Psalm 25:1–10
> 1 Thessalonians 3:9–13
> Luke 21:25–36
> Revelation 22:20

2.

In this season of bleak sun and chilling wind a voice of infinite warmth and tenderness is heard: "I shall comfort my people." It is God come to us in splendid mercy, in human form. Let God gather you as a shepherd sweeps up a lamb into his arms. There rest in joy. Let us worship the Good Shepherd who gathers us unto himself.

> 2nd Advent, Year B
> Isaiah 40:1, 11

3.

LEADER: As in days of old a fiery voice heralds the Savior's coming:

PEOPLE: "Prepare the way! Let all flesh prepare him room!"

LEADER: Christ is coming, Savior of love and light.
PEOPLE: He will find room and welcome in our hearts.
ALL: Come to us, Lord Jesus! Amen.

> 2nd Advent, Year C
> Malachi 3:1–4
> Luke 3:1–6

4.

LEADER: Rejoice with song, all people, for God's singing fills the
            heavens and earth!
PEOPLE: Let it be known in all the nations, God is our strength
            and song and salvation!
LEADER: God gathers us together for joy, to renew us in love. Let
            us rejoice with God in song!

> 3rd Advent, Year C
> Zephaniah 3:14–20
> Isaiah 12:2–6

5.

Friends, no less than upon Mary, God's favor and love rest upon
us. No less than to shepherds working by night, God bears light
into our darkness. Let us rejoice in God's gifts of love and light.
Amen.

> (Luke 1:26–31; 2:8–10)

6.

Friends, the God of tender mercy and forgiveness gives light to
those who sit in darkness and in the shadow of death. God guides
our feet into the way of peace. In prayer and with praise, let us
worship God together.

> (Luke 1:78–79, adapted)

7.

Prophets have announced it as a distant drumroll or peal of thunder. Angels have whispered it in dreams. But what was long kept
secret is now disclosed. Jesus said, "What I tell you in the dark,
utter in the light, and what you hear whispered, proclaim upon the
rooftops." So we proclaim, surely he comes soon! Let us worship
God together!

> 4th Advent, Year B
> (Matthew 10:27)
> Romans 16:25

8.
Come as a child to the kingdom!
Come believing in angels on heavenly errands,
    with eyes for a wandering star
    and ears for the message of dreams.
Come as a child who hears the angel proclaim,
    "With God all things are possible!"
Come as a child to the miraculous kingdom
    of the miraculous God!

> 4th Advent, Year B
> Luke 1:37
> (Mark 10:15)

9.
Have you kept watch through all the hours
like shepherds guarding their flock?
Are you listening to the angel message
borne quietly on the breeze?
The long watch is over; the Light has come
The Lord of the Advent, bearer of grace,
has appeared.
With all the angels let us praise his birth!

> Christmas Day, Year B
> Luke 2
> Titus 3:4

10.
Listen, I am a shepherd and I have news!
Go to Bethlehem, see what has happened!
A baby in a manger in a stable!
An odd place for a baby, an odder place yet for God!
Yet the angels told us, and we declare,
"This child shall bring God's favor and peace to all."
This is God's child, yet also ours!
Go to Bethlehem, see what has happened!
Like the child's mother, treasure all that you see and hear.
And like shepherds, rejoice in the God of wonder! Amen.

> Christmas
> Luke 2:1–20

11.
LEADER: Rejoice in the Lord! Let your hearts exult in God!
PEOPLE: For God has clothed us with the garments of salvation and covered us with the robe of goodness.
LEADER: As surely as the earth brings forth its fruit and the garden its blossoms,
PEOPLE: God has brought grace and redemption to all people!
ALL: Amen.

> 1st Sunday After Christmas, Year B
> Isaiah 61:10–11, adapted

PRAYERS OF PRAISE

1.
God, mysterious source of all life, we do not know when you will appear to us. Therefore, teach us vigilance. Give us the alertness to perceive your presence and to hear your call to serve. Jesus said, "The Son of man is coming at an hour you do not expect." Give to us such strength of faith that your nearness is no surprise any day or any hour. Amen.

> 1st Advent, Year A
> Matthew 24:36–44

2.
O Holy Christ, we wait for you, and you wait for us. We sense that you are near us, hidden in our lives in humble ways. We await the day when your power will stream forth and all will turn to face you, as you at all times face us. We tremble with the expectation of your advent. O guiding star, O morning sun, we raise our heads in awe, with song on our lips: our Redeemer draws near! Amen.

> 1st Advent, Year C
> Luke 21:25–36

3.
Eternal God, you make the vast silences of the universe tenderly alive with light and beauty; you bring light and mercy to those who silently, peacefully await your coming. The beauty of your presence fills the universe from humble human hearts to the farthest stars. With gratitude for the gift of light we praise you, God, for you lovingly encompass us this day and forever. Amen.

4.

O Christ, we watch and wait for the warmth and light of your presence. As candlelight is not overcome by darkness, we rejoice that your light is radiant within us, despite the wintry seasons of our lives. We live with hope that your birth will occur in every heart and the world will fall to its knees in joy. Amen.

(John 1:5)

5.

Dear God, Mary was told of Christ by Gabriel. The jealous heart of Herod spurred the Magi on their journey to the Christ child. The shepherds received the news by a midnight angels' chorus. We receive the news of his birth from Christ himself. At this hour, may he speak in our hearts, and may we, as calmly as Mary, accept his presence within us. Amen.

4th Advent, Year B
Luke 1:26–38

6.

Like a lavish angel you come, God, with light spilling from your hands, dispensing favor. And we who have labored long in darkness are so surprised, unaccustomed to your blessing, that our hearts pound in fear. When like a lavish angel you come, God, with peace spilling from your hands, may we, like Mary, accept you within us and, like the shepherds, embrace the Light shining in darkness. Then we will be filled with joy and wondering and hearts of holy calm. Amen.

4th Advent, Year B
Luke 1:26–31 (2:8–10)

7.

O Spirit of the Shepherd God,
Bend over us, as angels brushing low.
Open our eyes to the splendor!
Bid us rise to our feet,
as the shepherds rose out of fear,
rising into the peace and the favor of God.
O Spirit of the Shepherd God,
Bend over us, as angels brushing low.
Then send us, too, seeking Christ
in humble places. Amen.

Christmas Eve A,C
Christmas Day, Year A
Luke 2:8–20

8.
O Christ, Life of the World, you are born and your light is shed upon the earth. In you the desolate find comfort; the broken, healing; the hungry and thirsty, sustenance. You come to us, whatever our need, and pour God's power and love into our hearts. Christ, our Savior, find in us the welcome of Mary and Joseph, the shepherds' wonder and the angels' praise. Thanks be to God! Amen.

> Christmas
> (Luke 1:53)
> (Psalm 107:9)

9.
O Living Christ, we have waited so long for your birth. We yearn to shed the darkness that overshadows us. We long with people of all generations to be sheltered in your presence. Light of the World, Morning Sun—you break the hold of despair as you dawn in our hearts. In the warmth of your Light, we feel the love of God enfold us. It is no longer secret, no longer hidden: Christ has come! Christ is born! Love is loosed upon the world! Thank you, God, for this greatest of gifts! Amen.

> (Malachi 4:2)

10.
Great Shepherd of Souls, like the sudden brilliance of angels shining into sleepy shepherds' eyes, you bring us surprising mercy in the darkness. You lead us to ponder the treasures to be found in every humble circumstance, like that of the holy family lodged with animals bedded in straw. You lead us to ponder your hand in all mysteries and wonders, like Mary treasuring her child's birth and considering the bright future that can unfold from such a humble beginning. We praise you, God, for the gift of your Son, for such a treasure entrusted to our hands. Give us joy to proclaim the Savior's birth—the one in whom the world shall find life and peace. Amen.

> Christmas
> Luke 2:1–20

11.
O God, you are as young as a newborn child, yet ageless as the primordial waters, mountains, and plains. A thousand centuries

have not diminished your presence. With the intensity of the first creation you continue to press unfathomable splendor upon our inglorious lives. Immeasurably patient and loving, you feast us with an inexhaustible plenitude, filling the abyss of our hungers. This day you hallow all flesh, illuminating our birth, life, and death with the great light of your love. O God, newborn, yet ageless—with what promise and blessing you have graced this earth! Amen.

Christmas

12.

O God, we praise you for the birth of your child Jesus. He brings joy to our hearts, and we cherish him as deeply as those who first gazed upon his infant face. As we sense his spirit present in our hearts, we are aware that his life shall change our lives forever. As we trace the years of his life, we shall grow in patience and strength. As we see him bear frustration and defeat, we shall learn endurance and hope. As we see him show forth your glory, we shall be filled with the certainty of your saving presence. O God, who in love brought forth this child of grace, grant that we may grow with Jesus in all love and all wisdom. Amen.

1st Sunday After Christmas, Year B
Luke 2:22–40
Galatians 4:4–7

PRAYERS OF CONFESSION OR AFFIRMATION

1.

O Jesus, God's own Son, you came to earth as a child, to be cradled in all hearts. But we are unwilling guardians, unprepared to love one who makes demands on us at all hours. You ask that we receive God's love as a child, with trust and joy, but we are far too grown up to love without calculating the cost of your friendship. As you lived out your youth in Nazareth, maturing in grace and wisdom, you bid us realize that our lives are not yet complete and we are not mature. We confess our reluctance to admit that we have growing yet to do. O Jesus, Son of God, forgive us. Help us to become as children: astonished at grace, accepting of love, and hungry for maturity. Amen.

2.

God most merciful, had you not given your Son to us, we would be consumed with longing for a home we could not possess and tantalized by the promise of light shimmering at the horizon. By the advent of Christ into our lives, we possess a home where the heart finds shelter, and light to direct our journey. As we respond to your loving goodness, help us to draw others close to Christ, in whom all your promises find fulfillment. Amen.

> 1st Advent, Year C
> Affirmation
> (Deuteronomy 34:1–6)
> Luke 21:25–36

3.

Call to Confession: All we like sheep have strayed from the Good Shepherd. We have forsaken the Shepherd's voice, each following our own way. Let us ask for God's mercy.

> (Isaiah 53:6)
> (John 10:11–18)

O God, in Jesus Christ you have come as shepherd to your people, gathering us into one flock in reliance upon the Good Shepherd. We confess that we have refused to heed the call and to be guided to sources of nourishment and rest. We have assured ourselves that we have no need of protection from dangers without or within. We prefer to stray from the flock, from the support of people in community. O Great Shepherd, forgive us. Seek us out. Watch over us. Draw us unto yourself, in order that, trusting in your love, we may also trust the flock of those whom you gather to your side. Amen.

> 2nd Advent, Year B
> Isaiah 40:11
> (Psalm 23)
> (Ezekiel 34:16)

4.

God, with unhurried gentleness you draw near to us, bidding us lift our eyes to the infinite stars and open them to the ordinary wonders, numerous as snowflakes, all about us. Yet we see the waning sun, the snow upon the ground, the dazzle of holiday display, each other's weary faces, and we know that we have seen this all before. We cannot claim a breathless anticipation of the birth of your Son. From the prophet's good news to the shepherd's joyful witness, we have heard it all before. The season is familiar and holds no surprises for us. God, your power and love are ancient, yet ever new. Help us to see afresh the love borne into the world at each moment. Then with glad hearts may we welcome your Son, before whom even the desert blooms and rejoices. Amen.

> 3rd Advent, Year A
> Matthew 11:2–11
> Isaiah 35:1–10

5.

Call to Confession: In this Advent season, we each play a part in the unfolding drama of Jesus' birth. We are more likely to be found as harried, tense innkeepers than adoring shepherds at Jesus' side. Let us confess the sin which distances us from the love and worship of our Savior, and so leaves us unable to accommodate others' needs.

> (Luke 2:4–6, 7c)

God in whom all hearts find welcome, we confess that we have not yet made room in our hearts for the Christ child. We find the coming birth yet another event in our crowded lives. Like the harried innkeeper who had to refuse the couple a decent shelter, we find ourselves juggling people and obligations, torn between our compassion for the needy and the reality of what little we can do to bring comfort to all who ask of us. Like the innkeeper, we often relegate Christ to some out-of-the-way corner of our lives, without really intending to. Like Bethlehem at census time, we have little room for anything we haven't planned for. God, in whom all hearts find shelter, have mercy upon us. Help us, in the midst of our busy, burdened lives, to welcome the One who always has time for us. Amen.

> (Luke 2:4–6, 7c)

Assurance of Pardon: Our Savior says, "Let not your heart be troubled. . . . In my Father's house are many rooms. . . . I go to prepare a place for you . . . that where I am you may be also." Friends, the love of God is roomy, full of welcome. Know that you are forgiven; receive the welcome of God, where you will always find shelter. Amen.

> (John 14:1–3)

6.

O God, in all generations you have borne light into darkness. As a pillar of fire you gave guidance. From a burning bush you proclaimed deliverance. And in Christ you shed the light of mercy over all the earth. We confess that like shepherds we are fearful of the brightness of your glory. We find the vision of your majesty too much to bear. In your sublime presence we stand revealed. Our reluctance to love, our fear of being loved, our need of mercy, and our refusal to serve, all stand exposed. We are seen plainly as we are: sinners, lost, those sitting in darkness. Forgive our fear of your glory. Teach us to bear the Light and live in the peace by which you would bless all people. In Jesus' name we pray. Amen.

Christmas Eve, Year A
Luke 2:8–20

7.

God of wondrous mercy, as your Son is born, the exalted stars bend low in homage; humble ox and ass gaze upon him. The humble and the exalted are entwined in this child, our Savior. With Mary we treasure the birth of your Son; his birth gives us much to ponder. What do the squalor and the splendor of his birth portend? Shall he be King or Shepherd or both? What does the birth mean for us? Shall we, one distant day, grow up in grace, as he did? Shall we embody wondrous Spirit in a human frame? Shall our lives be a labor toward his birth within us? These are hard and mysterious questions, O God. As we celebrate his birth with delight, keep these questions before us. With solemn joy may we come to understand and treasure the grandeur of your Spirit poured into our humble lives! Amen.

Christmas
Affirmation
Isaiah 9:2–7
Luke 2:1–20

8.

In the fullness of time your Son is born, O God. This birth is the act that crowns all time in beauty and clothes the world in glory! We rejoice in his birth! Because Christ came to earth as an infant, our childhood reflects the light of God's favor. Because Christ grew in strength and wisdom, so we can grow in stature, wisdom, and love. As this child brought joy and a sense of completion to Simeon and Anna, we pray to know Jesus that we may live all our years with devotion and greet our death with peace. God, you have given us a heritage of divine power, the presence of grace, and the hope of eternal life. May we, like Simeon and Anna, declare your praise with gladness and peace! Amen.

1st Sunday After Christmas, Year B
Affirmation
Isaiah 61:10–62:3
Psalm 111
Galatians 4:4–7
Luke 2:22–44

PASTORAL PRAYERS

1.

Most Holy God, deep are the wounds of the people of the earth. Overwhelming are the tragedies of families and nations. Do you not see the rivers of tears? Do you not hear the cries of grief echoing from the earth's abyss? We are not strangers to grief or pain, loneliness or seasons of emptiness. But the burdens of the world, so unfathomably awful, we cannot bear. O God, the world and its people need you. We need you. Come, care for us as a forgiving father; comfort us as a mother bending over her child. Speak words of wisdom and guidance in the hearts of all your children, words of comfort and hope. And lest we, like errant children, fail to listen and so fail to live, bear with us in mercy until your kingdom comes and the world is one family.

2.

O Christ, you are the Good Shepherd of the earth. As sheep depend upon the love and guidance of their shepherd, we depend upon you to supply our needs. In your shepherding care, gather us to your side. There, in the flock of those who have heard your voice, give us nourishment for the labor of the day, peace for the evening hours, and rest for the night. In your love for all the world, you invite us, as you invited Peter, to feed your lambs and tend your flock. As we have found rest and refreshment in your presence, so enable us to shepherd others—giving protection, guidance, and nourishment to all people whom you would gather to yourself.

O Christ, all people are your flock, all the world is your pasture. Lift our eyes to the far horizons, that we might feel urgent, deep compassion for your weary world. As a shepherd cares for and knows each sheep by name, we now pray for those we love, and those we would love with your help. Lord, hear our prayer for all your people.

2nd Advent, Year B
Isaiah 40:11, 26
(John 10:11–16)
(John 21:15–19)

3.

O God, we have sown the seeds of our lives in anguish and tears, in the fervent hope that one will take root and cause our lives to bear fruit. Like the seeds of wheat that endure the dry season, waiting until they can sprout and grow, we endure the fruitless seasons of our lives. We dream of harvest, of the day when tears will cease and songs of joy will fill our hearts. You brought to birth the infant Savior, and you can surely cause our lives to flourish as well! O God, come quickly, bring a harvest of joy! Reap from the quiet fields of our lives a bounty of goodness, of mercy and justice. May all people know you as the God who restores wholeness to the broken, as mighty a work as leveling the mountains or raising up the meadow to the mountain summit. O God, come quickly, fill our hearts with laughter and joy!

2nd Advent, Year C
Psalm 126
Luke 3:1–6

4.

O God, we are too wise and too old to change our ways, to turn and become as children. Children snuggle in their beds, anticipating presents, while we anticipate their cost. They sing of peace on earth; we are concerned about war. The world is too much with us, and we know too much about it to return to our years of innocence. How then shall we receive a Savior who is bundled in infant's clothes? Jesus said, "Turn and become as children." He said to be born anew. So we pray for fresh beginnings—the birth of hope, the rebirth of wonder, the growth of love. We pray that Christ's birth will renew our lives and rekindle our hope in the world.

(Matthew 18:3)
(John 3:3)

5.

Prayer of the Innkeeper

O God, the night is so dark and the inn so full.
As my guests prepare for their night's rest,
a couple lingers outside, hoping for welcome.
What can I do for them? There is no room here.
I cannot turn my guests out of their beds.
And I cannot hope that a guest will relinquish his room.
It is up to me to provide the couple shelter,
up to me to welcome them.
I will give them what I have (and that's not much)
and hope that it will suffice.
I will help these strangers, and perhaps,
in some unforeseen way, angels will bless my way.
Good God, in whom all souls find rest and room and board,
bless all people. Bless all who make hard decisions,
weighing expedience and compassion, and, with your help,
may compassion prevail!

(Luke 2:4–6, 7c)
(Hebrews 13:2)

6.

God of holy peace, we are accustomed to the darkness of our world, accustomed to tragedy, sorrow, and worry. Like the shepherds sitting in darkness, expecting nothing, we are familiar with dim hope. Yet we brood over our troubled lives and world, wondering when you will come in power to bring unassailable peace to all hearts and all lands. Break the hold of darkness, God, and let your peace dawn in our hearts! Look with favor upon your people and grant us your blessing. And should angels intercept us with clear messages of your intent for our lives, should angels shower your radiance before us like the falling snow, let us with wonder accept your love as the generous gift that it is.

7.

Holy God, Mover of the earth and Anchor of our souls, you never give up on us. Why is it that you will not let us go? Who would have thought that divine power could care for us? Again and again we refuse to listen to your voice; we close the door on opportunities you open; we ignore and deny you; we refuse the shelter of your strength. And yet you affirm us and persist in giving us good gifts.

Your love is not tame, God. Your love surges—wave upon wave of light and mercy, breaking upon us. You knock at the door of our consciousness. You search out the one lost coin, the lost sheep, the one person yet out in the cold. You urge us to persistent and bold prayer. And time after time, you bring miracle, wonder, and healing, teaching us to expect your overwhelming love.

If we have resisted your love in any way, Holy God, open us to your power. Let Christ be born in our hearts and turn us to face the Light.

(Psalm 8)
(Luke 15)

8.

Most Holy God, with the astonished shepherds we praise you for all that we have seen and heard concerning the holy child Jesus. He is God-with-us, the abiding mystery of the divine Spirit, woven into our lives. We thank you, God, for Jesus Christ. He comes to teach, to heal, and to save us. He comes as light in our darkness. He comes as a shepherd to protect and guide us. We are drawn irresistibly to this Savior through whom the love and mercy of God are poured into our lives. We thank you for this Christmas Day: for the joy of family, of gift-giving and feasting. Open our hearts in gratitude, O God, that we may love all people as Christ. Hear us as we give thanks for those whom we cherish and all that gives us delight.

Christmas

9.

O God, gentle as dream and splendid as angel song, your voice sounds through the sky. To shepherds watching in darkness, your splendor flares. Come to us, who also watch and wait in darkness, weary and unexpectant. Bless our lives with light and bathe the world with peace.

The vision of chanting angels will quickly fade. So as the shepherds came in haste, bring us quickly to Jesus' side. And, as certain as the shepherds, let us proclaim: This is the Savior!

Lest this day pale and vanish, like Mary let us ponder all these things, turning to the promise of his birth: that this is he who shall bring us light and peace.

O Father of all mercies and Mother of all comfort, send your blessing of peace into all the world and upon all whom we name in the silence of prayer.

Christmas
Luke 2:1–20

10.

O God, in the life of Jesus we see how gradually divinity unfolds within human life. You were in no hurry, God. You worked through that hidden life at Nazareth with patience and faith in the pace of human maturation. If you were assured that the infant Jesus would eventually display the fullness of the promise present at his birth, then teach us to see the potential within our lives and to acknowledge that our full maturity may require a lifetime. Like fruit ripening upon the vine or wine mellowing into full flavor, our fruition requires a long duration.

Deliver us, God, from the impatience that would arrest our growth, settling for a partial fulfillment of our potential. Deliver us, God, from haste in judging the meaning of others' lives. For even your own Son evidenced his promise rather late. Grant us patience and trust in your providence, working for mercy and for justice, all in the fullness of your time.

1st Sunday After Christmas, Year B
Luke 2:22–40

EPIPHANY

CALLS TO WORSHIP

1.

Christ is born! Like the Magi, take your bearing from the star, led by mystery and the deepest yearnings of your hearts. Like the Magi, offer the infant Savior your treasure, the best of your gifts. Let us worship God together! Amen.

> Epiphany A,B,C
> Isaiah 60:1–6
> Matthew 2:1–12

2.

The Christ child is born!
All you who would find him,
prepare for a journey, determined as the Magi.
All you who would praise him,
come with the faith to follow but a star.
All you who would worship him,
come with humility to the child
who shows forth the immeasurable riches of God!

> Epiphany A,B,C
> Matthew 2:1–12

3.

LEADER: The Lord reigns over the waters! God creates life from primeval waters, grants safe passage through troubled waters, heals and refreshes us with living waters.

PEOPLE: The river of God flows, carrying us toward the ocean of mercy.

LEADER: Let us worship God, source of life!

ALL: Amen.

> Baptism of the Lord A,B,C
> Psalm 29

4.

LEADER: As at the first creation, God calls us from chaos and darkness into the light of birth.

PEOPLE: "The voice of the Lord is upon the waters," calling us to be immersed in the Spirit, as those baptized into grace and reborn in mercy.

LEADER: Come to the river of God's grace. Let us worship God who buoys us with unending streams of love. Amen.

Baptism of the Lord A,B,C
Psalm 29

5.

LEADER: In your presence, God, there is fullness of joy!

PEOPLE: We are brimful, like Cana's jars, touched by the Savior's hand.

LEADER: In God's presence there is joy like that of a family celebrating a wedding.

ALL: With joy we worship our Lord! Amen.

2nd Epiphany, Year C
(Psalm 16:11b)
John 2:1–11

6.

People of God, as Jesus astonished the people of Galilee with his teaching and the miracle of his healing grace, so he would work among us, surprising us with joy. Let us worship God, celebrating the graciousness of divine mercy.

4th Epiphany, Year B
Mark 1:21–28

7.

LEADER: Lay down your work and ascend the mountain. With attentive prayer, look to Jesus.

PEOPLE: At the summit, we see he is more than we thought. The light is not an apparition, not the play of sunlight on snow.

LEADER: Jesus is the Christ, cloaked in mystery, majestic in splendor, the Light of God, illuminating all of life. Listen to him!

PEOPLE: It is good to be here, worshiping our Lord. His light transfigures our existence.

ALL: Amen.

Transfiguration, Year B
Mark 9:2–9

8.

LEADER: We await our Savior. We gather on the mountain and with open eyes behold him.

PEOPLE: We receive strength to live in the valley.

LEADER: God's love is revealed in the face of Christ. With unveiled faces we behold his glory.

PEOPLE: His splendor is unfading, the power of his love is undiminished.

LEADER: To us the gift of God has been revealed: God's Son, the Chosen One.

ALL: We listen and worship, for Christ is here. Amen.

> Transfiguration, Year C
> Luke 9:28–36
> 2 Cor. 3:12–4:2 (6)

PRAYERS OF PRAISE

1.

God of all who wander, we have come through many deserts; we have endured them all. And now we see the Light that the Holy Child sheds upon our path. We worship him, offering the treasure of our hearts. God, be our guiding light. Dispel all darkness, and let the good news shine in our lives in word and deed. Amen.

> Epiphany A,B,C
> Matthew 2:1–12

2.

We praise you, God, for love that endures, as the fragile infant Jesus survived the bumbling Magi spilling their news, the wrath of Herod, and the rough journey into a foreign land. We thank you, God, for love that withstands our assaults, intended or not. Help us always to trust that your love will survive mightily in our hearts as well. Amen.

> Epiphany A,B,C
> Matthew 2:1–12

3.

O Christ, we gather to adore you.
For the splendor of your birth
and the brightness of your glory
have not been dimmed by all the ages.
We raise a song of praise,
proclaiming youɪ mercy to all the world. Amen.

> Epiphany

4.

God of mystery, at every turning point in Joseph's life you spoke, directing him to safety and refuge. As you spoke to him, you speak to us. Your voice sounds in the depths of our being, as constant as a flowing stream. We need only become still to hear it. In this hour, still the voices that distract us, that we may hear clearly your divine intent in our lives. Amen.

(Matthew 1:18–25; 2:13–23)

5.

We praise you, God, for the mysteries of water: blanketing the earth with snowy peace, washing the air, cleansing the earth with rain, rising in mists like incense, flowing in soft currents which join in rivulets to the mighty ocean, slaking our thirst and giving us life. We praise you, God, for your Spirit poured into our lives, as plentiful as the waters. The Spirit gives us birth, refreshes us, gives us provision for the journey through all desert regions. For the gift of water we praise you, God! Amen.

Baptism of the Lord

6.

Spirit of Power, in every age you give transforming power—converting chaos to creation, Sarai to Sarah, Abram to Abraham, Saul to Paul, water to wine, and death to life. In every age, you beckon your people to become new creatures. We praise you for showing the possibility of great change and the hope for your mercy touching human lives! Amen.

2nd Epiphany, Year C
Isaiah 62:1–5
John 2:1–11

7.

O Christ, you have not hidden your glory from our eyes. You first showed forth God's presence at a wedding feast in a simple home. And we can discern your light in the silences of prayer. If you transformed humble water into wine, you can transform us, too. Remake us until we too brim over with the joy of your presence. Amen.

2nd Epiphany, Year C
John 2:1–11

8.

With love as fresh as the winter air and pristine as newly fallen snow you bless our lives, O God. Like a blanket of snow you wrap a mantle of peace about us, protecting us from savage winter winds. We praise you, O God, for love as blessed as sun in the depths of winter. Grant us the grace to take shelter in your Spirit, and the compassion to draw inside those confronted by all harsh elements. Amen.

9.

Yours, O God, is the sweep of the prairie—the sun, the wind, the rain, the snow. Yours is the turning of the seasons, yours the villages scattered across it. Your hand creates the crystal snow, seeds of grain, and all the flowers. We praise you for all daily graces. But may we not seek you in these wonders alone; attune our hearts to the quiet miracles of love and friendship, the satisfaction of generous service, and the strength of your presence. Keep us, your servants, ever ready to sing your praise, always eager to serve as you call and guide us. In Jesus' name we pray. Amen.

10.

O Living Christ, in each and every person you come to meet us. Behind the steady pace of our lives, beneath the noise and detail, you dwell in an inner sanctuary which we call our soul. At this still point, this quiet and holy place, you spread your arms, creating an unassailable tranquillity. You bid us enter to quench our thirst for all that is holy in life. Always you stand and bid us enter this interior peace. In this hour, renew us by your Spirit and your presence. Amen.

11.

Of all the currents that sway us, yours, Lord, is the deepest, the most steadfast. From womb to old age and beyond, we are carried in your strong arms. For your constant presence, we give you praise. For your constant guidance, we give you thanks. For your love and mercy without ceasing, we lift a song in our hearts and worship you with reverence and trust. Amen.

(Isaiah 46:3–4)

12.

Most wondrous God, from the beginning you have found delight in all your creatures. You declare your work to be good. As we

seek your presence here, God, open our hearts to receive your
affirming love. Then send us forth to uphold others, with whom
we share communion in your love. Amen.

(Genesis 1)

13.

To each of us, God, you make available a love unfathomable in
its depth, incredible in its intensity. This morning help us to be
more open to its power. Then help us, as followers of Christ, to
bear your love into the world. Raise in our hearts exultation,
wonder, and thanksgiving for all that you give and all that you ask
of us. Amen.

14.

Holy God, Giver of Life, we acknowledge that your love is as
constant as a river's flow, brimming with abundance and power.
And we know that to receive your Spirit we must be cut like
channels, open to your currents. But the process is tedious, age-
long; our transformation is slow. It takes many years for us to
learn to receive the great wash of your love without resistance.
Nevertheless, labor within us. Shape us as channels of your vitality, that in the clarity of wisdom we may know that before the
earth was, you were; and before we were conscious of ourselves,
you were laboring within us, to bring us to our second birth.
Amen.

15.

O Christ, as men and women of ancient Galilee crowded about
you with joy and wonder, recognizing the Spirit of God in your
words and your touch, we too praise you for words of healing and
promise and for your presence, interceding in our lives. Grant us
unwavering devotion to your Spirit, that we may always praise
your name and that the world may receive your present healing
power. Amen.

7th Epiphany, Year B
Mark 2:1–12

16.

God of glory, few of us will ever catch a glimpse of your splendor,
which is brighter than the sun. But Jesus comes to each of us, as
he came to the disciples. He brings healing with his touch,

strength with his encouragement, and the peace that banishes all fear. Thus let Christ be among us today. Amen.

Transfiguration, Year A
Matthew 17:1–9

17.
Lord of the winter, we praise you for the snows and storms of winter. They force us to seek shelter and offer quiet to us. In this hard and barren season, you lead us to the riches of silence. If we are calm enough, peaceful in heart, we find Jesus our Christ—hear him or see him dwelling in unfathomable light brighter than sun or snow. May we linger in the peace of his presence, until he bids us follow him upon the earth, for the sake of his creation. Amen.

Transfiguration, Year B
Mark 9:2–9

18.
Holy God, we offer you praise for the rigors of your love. As harsh winters enforce silence and rest, your harder demands summon us to that portion of faith usually ignored. Like the disciples with Jesus upon the holy mountain, we realize again the discipline required for prayer, the necessity for guidance from the past to direct the future, the urgency of listening to your voice. All praise be to you, O God, for austere mercies recalling us to the essentials of our faith. Amen.

Transfiguration, Year C
Luke 9:28–36

PRAYERS OF CONFESSION OR AFFIRMATION

1.
O God, the Magi endured a harsh journey in their search for the Christ. His birth inconvenienced his parents, Joseph and Mary, finally forcing their exile from everything familiar. We confess that we do not think of your Son exacting a sacrifice from us, but selflessness is what he expects. The child Jesus brought turbulence into the world, but we confess that we have fled from seeking him in troubled places and people. O God, we resent the inconvenience, the demands, the change of plans that the birth of your Son brings into our comfortable lives. In your mercy, forgive us. And prepare our hearts to follow Christ, even into a far and foreign country. Amen.

Epiphany
Matthew 2:1–12 (13–33)

2.

Call to Confession: Infants always evoke reactions. God, too, is young, lying cooing in a simple cradle, and already people respond: He kindles the hearts of the Magi to love, and Herod is incensed with violence. As we worship the Christ child this day, let us confess aloud and in silence our responses to his birth.

Matthew 2:1–16

God of the Bethlehem star, everyone is searching for your Light, shining in the face of Christ. The Magi sought Christ simply to worship him. But Herod sought him to appease his jealous anger. We confess that our motives in seeking Jesus are not pure. We do not come simply to worship: we come to Christ, asking his benefits of reassurance, health, wealth; asking him to fulfill the hundred petitions for not-so-important requests that we heap before him. But, the Magi sought first the kingdom. Help us, God, to follow their example, putting our own need in perspective, worshiping the Christ in love, content to be in your presence, and laying our gifts before you. Then may we journey, trusting that your goodness and light will accompany us all the days of our life. Amen.

Epiphany A,B,C
Matthew 2:1–12 (13–16)
(Matthew 6:33)

3.

God of all flesh, in Jesus Christ you have immersed divine splendor and wisdom into human life. He is not repelled by the shabbiness and shamefulness of our lives, but seeks to redeem us. We confess our repulsion from those whose actions bewilder us, whose sorrow burdens us, or whose good fortune somehow detracts from our lives. Our compassion is limited to those like ourselves. Our kindness is reserved for those kind to us. Our passionate concern remains silent until our own little kingdoms are threatened. O God, forgive us. Cleanse us of self-centeredness, and open us to the whole breadth and length, height and depth of your love, manifest in all creation. Amen.

Baptism of the Lord, Year B
Mark 1:4–11

4.

O God, you delight in creation. You did not create the earth for sorrow nor humanity for sadness. You made us for joy! When we verge on despair, you approach without fanfare, transforming our weary mutterings into joyous song! You did not want to see the world torn with grief, bereft of song or reasons to sing. Therefore you sent your Son to enter our days, as he graced the wedding at Cana—quietly, with joy brimming over. Jesus attends our feasts and festivities, desires that we celebrate each other, and in our joy remember you, O God, source of all refreshment. We give you thanks, God, for this good news. Amen.

> 2nd Epiphany, Year C
> Affirmation
> John 2:1–11

5.

Holy God, we confess that we are the poor in spirit, those who mourn, those who hunger and thirst for justice. Yet we have no hope of blessing; the reality of heaven and comfort and justice is far from us today: for recent tragedy has numbed us to any blessing that life might carry. We think also of the private burdens of sickness, trouble, and grief suffered by those we know, and we question, God, your power to save, to heal, to bring life out of death. Have mercy upon us, God, for we cannot see beneath our sorrow. Gently bring healing to our hearts, forgiving us as you strengthen us to live with joy once more. Amen.

> 4th Epiphany, Year C
> Matthew 5:1–12

6.

God, forgive our doubting, questioning hearts. Like the Scribes who witnessed Jesus' miracles of healing and heard his proclamation, yet spurned belief, we too have seen wonders, yet have hardened our hearts. We confess the many times our pessimism has caused others to doubt themselves and your Spirit, the times that our criticism has wounded others and that our dejection has dampened the enthusiasm of those inspired by your word and work. O God, forgive us, and in your mercy renew us, that with open hearts we may believe and never pose an obstacle to the faith of others. Amen.

> 7th Epiphany, Year B
> Mark 2:1–12

7.

Lord of the just and the unjust, we confess that your ways puzzle us and your commands are difficult. It is not easy to bless those who insult us and to pray for those who abuse us. You summon us to love the ungrateful and the selfish, just as we love those who are kind and generous. This too is a hard demand. In your mercy, God, forgive us. For we have cursed those who have cursed us; we have heaped scorn on the selfish, rather than love. Deliver us from bitterness. Rescue us from resignation. And lift us from despair to hope and trust in your mercy and justice. Amen.

7th Epiphany, Year C
Luke 6:27–38

8.

Most amazing God, the mystery of your radiance surrounds us. Like the disciples of Jesus, we confess our unease with transcendent mystery. Faced with your splendor, we do not take time for attentive silence, as Jesus did, but evade the holy with stammering and busyness—anything to avoid your power. We also confess those times when we are at ease with holiness, absorbed in prayer and thought, but so in love with your love that we neglect those in need. As Jesus descended to the valley to work among the poor of the earth, so direct us to our responsibilities. Such is the mystery of your love, O God, which both overwhelms and attracts us. Have mercy upon us and forgive us. Free us to love and serve in equal measure. Amen.

Transfiguration, Year B
Mark 2:2–9

9.

LEADER: Revealer of Mystery, like weary disciples stirred from their sleep, we too find Christ waking us, offering a vision more wonderful than any dream.

PEOPLE: We have preferred our sleep to your splendor, O God.

LEADER: Unaccustomed to your splendor, we too find it difficult to listen to your voice.

PEOPLE: We have not listened, O God.

LEADER: As the disciples were overwhelmed by your light and missed the purpose of Jesus' prayer, we too are bedazzled by signs of your presence, missing their intent: to bring us into closer obedience to your will.

PEOPLE· We have not followed you, O God.

LEADER: Have mercy upon us, God, unconscious of your radiance, underestimating the demands you make upon us.
ALL: Amen.

> Transfiguration, Year C
> Luke 9:28–36
> (Daniel 2:47)

PASTORAL PRAYERS

1.

Luminous Spirit in whom all life finds direction, when you hovered over the waters, you brought life to earth. Bringing Noah and his family through the flood, you gave humanity a fresh beginning. Bearing the infant Christ into the world, you gave us a new understanding of what it means to love all creation passionately. Everywhere, your world cries out for a fresh beginning—nations, families, individuals. All need your direction, your justice, your mercy. Hear the plea of your people, O God.

Help us to find our way back to Jesus' side, making the journey through personal sadness and national tragedy, into the good Light of your presence. As you led the Magi unerringly to Jesus, give us, also, a bright star of hope for direction and endurance. Lighten our way, O God, and guide all nations and all hearts on the path leading to your presence.

> Epiphany A,B,C
> Matthew 2:1–12
> Isaiah 60:1–6

2.

God, source of mercy, we come before you, as stubborn as Naaman—broken, blighted, at once tolerant of and impatient with our disease. We seek out healing, as long as the cure is something we can understand. But we are unwilling to do the simple, mysterious things through which you will draw near to cleanse us. Have mercy upon us, O God, for we cannot fathom your ways and how simply you call to us.

As you hovered over the waters and wrought the beauty of creation with your voice, draw near to us, who are in deep waters. Call us forth washed, renewed, restored to the beauty and integrity of your first creation. As you drew forth Naaman from the Jordan with flesh restored like the flesh of a young child, you can remake us anew, O God. And thus restored, with joy and love, untainted as a child's, we would serve you all our days. We lift this prayer not only for ourselves, but for the people of the world, whom you call to yourself through our Savior, Jesus Christ.

> Baptism of the Lord, Year B
> Genesis 1:1–5
> (2 Kings 5:1–15)

3.

God, most Ancient of Days, between the dawn of childhood and the door of death, many things happen to us. Caught in day-to-day events, we lose sight of our miraculous origins, our mysterious departure, and the common thread that draws our entire lives together—your presence and love. As we grow wiser and more mature, as we become more loving and self-giving, you do not abandon us, as if we had become self-sufficient. Your care is always available to us, replenishing us for love. We trust your words, "Even to your old age I am your God, and to gray hairs I will carry you." Thank you, God, for your presence through our entire lives.

> (Isaiah 46:4)

4.

God of light, wellspring of inexhaustible energy, exuberance, and love, we are here because our hope is dulled by habit, our vision is dimmed by contentment. We seek the vitality and the strength derived from a fresh sense of your nearness and your hope for us. We have been content with limited horizons; we expect only the commonplace: sickness, tragedy, frustration, ignorance. We do not expect the miraculous and the sacred, joy and creative strength. We acknowledge that this is how we are: awake to life's crudeness and asleep to its holiness. O God, never let us close our minds to the varied ways in which you can reach us. Grant us great expectations, openness, and vigilance, that we may say, "Speak, Lord, for your servant hears."

> 2nd Epiphany, Year B
> 1 Samuel 3:1–10

5.

Lord, somehow we always find that your abundant mercy more than meets our need. If we look back on the hard times, we find that you filled our empty lives with grace. We have seen sickness and grief. We have been far from those we love in their time of need, and have been unable to help. We have endured all kinds of unfortunate circumstances. Because our sorrow grieves you as much as it does us, we know that you seek to strengthen us through hardship. You use the empty place within us as a chalice which you fill not with tears, but with new wine, a renewed sense of joy in life. We offer ourselves now, in silent prayer, to the working of your Spirit.

2nd Epiphany, Year C
John 2:1–11

6.

O God, you alone fathom the way of the sea. Your people are like ocean fish—aware only of water, the depths, danger, and hidden places. Immersed in our lives, we cannot fathom change or any other way of living, unless we are lifted up, gathered into the world of light by the hand of Christ. We know the ways of darkness, the depths of soul devoid of joy and hope and light. You have given us joy. You have lifted us up. Thus we rejoice in the one who has shown us the light, giving us the assurance that love exists in the world. As we gain trust in your light and wisdom, God, we learn that mercy received carries responsibility to those still submerged in darkness. As you called the disciples, so you call us to help you draw up the hopeless out of despair. Therefore we cast our nets, rejoicing as we lift up the hopeless into the light of Christ.

3rd Epiphany, Year A
Isaiah 9:1–4
Matthew 4:12–23

7.

O Christ, it is no wonder that in every age men and women catch a glimpse of your splendor and become your followers. Though we are among the least of all people, common folk bearing no great distinction, you stand at the threshold of our lives with the promise that our barren lives can yield unexpected grace. Even though we have labored through long and fruitless hours, though we claim no talent and feel unworthy to bear your love into the world, you still call, pouring the fullness of divine care into such unwitting vessels as we are. As you directed the disciples to a great catch of fish, you can wrest forth a surprising harvest from our lives as well. O Christ, may your gracious promise to us not be in vain. Grant us openness and eagerness to follow you and to show forth God's glory to the world.

5th Epiphany, Year C
Isaiah 6:1–8
1 Corinthians 15:1–11
Luke 5:1–11

8.
Living God, where do you get your energy?
As if the continuous creation of the universe is not enough,
you are also active among us, mending broken hearts,
restoring hope, reconciling us to each other.
Your strength never fails!
In this season of cold days and long nights,
we are tempted to hibernate, to withdraw
into a warm, safe place.
We need to recoup our strength and reorganize our priorities.
Our inner fire needs to be fed.
You, Lord, are the only source from which we
can draw the strength we need.
Come to us in this season of hidden growth.
Help us to get our house back in order,
to listen to your word to us
that we may attend to the work of your church
with renewed zest.
God, invigorate us with the vitality of the Spirit.
Energize us with your love.
Equip us with power to serve you,
and help us to seize this day with exultation!

9.
Lord of all that is silent and all that is spoken: because our lives
are full of detail and deadlines, much to be done and little time
in which to do it all, we find few moments in which to savor the
beauty of the world, to contemplate the fierce endurance of everything that lives, to enter that timeless realm of divine mystery
which surrounds us, entered only in silence. Yet we know that this
place exists and is close to us. O God, grant us a glimpse of this
inner sanctuary, and the desire and calm to dwell there in prayer.
As Jesus was cloaked in mystery and transfigured in light, labor
over us, until we too are transformed, reborn in light, at peace in
the Spirit.

Transfiguration, Year B
Mark 9:2–9

10.
Forgive, O God, the oblivion in which we hide our timid hearts.
Wrapped in forgetfulness like slumber, we are unaware of the
good, the evil, the suffering and the beauty all about us. As Moses

did not know that he shone with your light, so we are unaware of the times when our lives are signs of your presence to others. Yet from time to time we flare, unknowing, with the ancient light, and those who gaze upon us know the reality of your presence.

Like Jesus' disciples who were asleep when he needed them, we too have failed close friends who sought our company for strength. But we were unaware of all that they were suffering, and, thinking that all was well, we slept. Forgive us, God, for our failure to support those who have needed us.

We have shielded ourselves, God, from the evil of the world. As we seek to protect ourselves from the pain it inflicts, our isolation also prevents us from taking the first steps toward healing and justice. Forgive us, God, for evil flourishes when we seek to forget its terrors.

Forgive us too, God, for failing to sense the beauty of your world and its creatures. Numbed by our labors and caring, we fail to observe the splendors that surround us. Yet a child's innocent smile, winter fields of snow, the quiet power of a winding river all are windows into the beauty of your love.

Waken us afresh, O God, to goodness, to the reality of evil, the pain of suffering, and the beauty of your creation. Then may we serve you with urgency, knowing full well the necessity of your saving love in our world.

Transfiguration, Year C
Exodus 34:29–35
Luke 9:28–36

LENT

CALLS TO WORSHIP

1.
LEADER: The disciples asked Jesus, "Lord, teach us to pray."
PEOPLE: So we also ask the Lord to teach us how to pray.
LEADER: Paul said, "You must help us by prayer."
PEOPLE: Prayer is our duty, our deepest and highest calling.
LEADER: God declared to Solomon, "My eyes will be open and my ears attentive to the prayer that is made in this place."
PEOPLE: God is attentive to us here. Therefore we worship the Lord with joy, listening for God's word in our lives.

> (Matthew 6:9)
> (2 Corinthians 1:11)
> (2 Chronicles 7:15)

2.
LEADER: The God of mercy tends to our needs,
PEOPLE: Leading us out of the wilderness, up from the depths, out of darkness.
LEADER: As gracious as the dawn to those longing for light,
PEOPLE: So welcome is the Lord's love to those who have endured in trust and hope.
ALL: Amen.

> 1st Lent, Year A
> Psalm 130
> Matthew 4:1–11

3.
LEADER: Let us be led by the Spirit,
PEOPLE: Even if the path to the promised land leads straight through the desert,

2/23/97

LEADER: Through hunger and doubt and temptation;
PEOPLE: Even if we are led where we would rather not go.
LEADER: Yet we will be led by the Spirit
PEOPLE: And end our journey rejoicing in the Lord our God.
ALL: Amen.

> 1st Lent, Year C
> Deuteronomy 26:1–11
> Psalm 91:9–16
> Luke 4:1–13
> (John 21:18–19)

4.

LEADER: Friends, you are sons of Abraham and daughters of Sarah, heirs of God's blessing and covenant.
PEOPLE: May we too walk in God's presence, trusting in the guidance of God.
LEADER: Know that God's chosen ones find divine power beyond all human comprehension and God's ways mysterious, miraculous.
PEOPLE: Then may we live and worship with the strong faith of Abraham and Sarah, open to God's call and presence. Amen.

> 2nd Lent, Year B
> Genesis 17:1–19

5.

LEADER: Steadfast in purpose, God in Christ calls to us,
PEOPLE: Offering protection from the night, and love that empowers for the day.
LEADER: Christ longs to draw us close,
PEOPLE: That we may know his love overflowing with strength and tenderness,
LEADER: Love intent on embracing the world.
ALL: Responding to his call, we draw close to Christ. Amen.

> 2nd Lent, Year C
> Luke 13:31–35

6.

People of God, as our Creator spoke to the Hebrews saying, "I am the Lord your God," so God lays claim to us in a bond of love. As God summoned the people to the holy mountain, so does he still summon us to gather in worship, to hear his voice. Let each of you affirm God's love, declaring in your heart, "Speak, Lord, for your servant hears." Let us worship God.

3rd Lent, Year B
Exodus 20:1–21

7.

LEADER: God, who is rich in mercy, out of great love gives us life through Christ,

PEOPLE: That in the coming ages God might show the immeasurable riches of divine grace in kindness toward us in Christ.

LEADER: By grace we have been saved through faith. It is not our doing; it is the gift of God.

ALL: In thanksgiving, we lift our hearts in worship.

4th Lent, Year B
Ephesians 2:4–10, adapted

8.

Come to the Light; be gathered to Christ! Christ dwells in our midst, as the Light not overcome in darkness, as the Shepherd gathering us home from every place of exile and distress. He is the gift of God who cherishes us with unspeakable love! Come to the Light; be gathered to Christ! Let us worship God, the Giver of Life. Amen.

4th Lent, Year B
John 3:14–21

9.

LEADER: Brothers and sisters, come back from the far country, from the exile of self-contempt, or the fields of dutiful labor.

PEOPLE: For God longs to welcome and love us!

LEADER: God weighs neither the sad detours of our journey nor our cheerless attempts to earn favor.

PEOPLE: We who have been lost are found in the embrace of God's arms. We are found when we forgive each other, and seal our peace with joy!

LEADER: Let us worship God who awaits our return with lavish love.

ALL: Amen.

4th Lent, Year C
Luke 15:1–3, 11–32

10.

LEADER: Like those who worshiped with the disciples long ago,
PEOPLE: We too wish to see Jesus.
LEADER: Know that Christ is true to his promise;
PEOPLE: Having died and risen, he has drawn all people to himself.
ALL: In his presence we find our joy and salvation. Amen.

> 5th Lent, Year B
> Psalm 51:10–17
> John 12:20–33

11.

As spring approaches, the earth emerges from the silence and rest of winter. God calls all creation to wake and stretch to new growth. Let us praise God who renews us for love and service. Amen.

> 5th Lent, Year C
> Isaiah 43:16–21
> John 12:1–8
> Philippians 3:8–14

12.

LEADER: Rejoice, friends of God! For your King comes to you triumphant in love, and humbled as a servant.
PEOPLE: Hosanna to the Son of David! Blessed is he who comes in the name of the Lord!
LEADER: We proclaim Jesus Christ of Nazareth as our Lord and Savior.
PEOPLE: And we follow him, the Way to everlasting life and peace. Amen.

> Palm Sunday, Year A
> (Zechariah 9:9)
> Matthew 21:1–11

13.

The great entrance is prepared.
In the olive grove, leaves are still and the wind is hushed.
In reverence they welcome the Messiah.
Silently he rides the beast of burden and peace
into Jerusalem.
As he draws near, the silence melts into joyful clamor.
This is he who has made the blind see, the lame walk,
the dead live!

The Messiah is in our midst!
With the joyful throng and the joyful earth
let us praise Christ our King! Amen.

> Palm Sunday, Year C
> Luke 19:28–40

14.

The Lord is gracious to those in distress and sustains those who are weary. Having assumed human form in Jesus our Christ, God understands our sorrows and our strengths as one who has endured the greatest violence, yet rose into everlasting strength and joy. Let us worship the Lord whose compassion was borne in enduring the cross. Amen.

> Passion Sunday A,B,C
> (Also Good Friday A,B,C)
> (Isaiah 52:13–53:12)
> (Isaiah 40:28–31)

15.

People of God, you are those whom Christ calls his friends; friends with whom he shares the depths of his life. Break bread with him who loves you. Pray with him in his distress. Stand by him at the hour of his death. We can do no less for the friend who has laid down his life for us. Amen.

> Maundy Thursday A,B,C
> (John 15:13–14)

16.

LEADER: Come, let us return to the Lord.
PEOPLE: We are torn; God will heal us.
LEADER: We are stricken; God will bind us up.
PEOPLE: God will revive us and raise us up that we may live before him.
LEADER: "Let us press on to know the Lord; his going forth is sure as the dawn;
PEOPLE: "He will come to us as the showers, as the spring rains that water the earth."
ALL: Amen.

> (Hosea 6:1–3, adapted)
> (Good Friday)

PRAYERS OF PRAISE

1.
O God, we thank you for the signs that life continues; for brave crocuses rising from their winter graves, for the rains that nourish the fields, for the return of birds whose call wakes the day with praise. More than these, we cherish the promises of Jesus which grace our hearts like the spring sun. Because he lives, we also shall live. Fairest Lord Jesus, come visit us this day. Amen.

2.
O Spirit, shepherd of our growth, just as the endurance of winter produces a certain hardiness within us and a greater appreciation of spring, so does endurance of uncertainty and trouble force a strengthening of faith, a growth of spiritual courage, and greater compassion toward those whose trials have been far harsher than ours. We praise you, God, for our times of trouble. Had our journey been carefree, we might not know the fullness of your love which spans the heights of our joy to the depths of our sorrow. Amen.

1st Lent, Year C
Luke 4:1–13

3.
O God, the light of all the stars is but a pale glimmer in your vast ocean of light. We praise you for mysteries we cannot comprehend; for your gracious, gentle will working through everything that lives to form a holy people. Yours alone is the scope to comprehend how all our separate lives and desires cohere into a grand pattern, reflecting your design. O God, though we know little about your ways, work through us that your will be done, not ours; and that one day all the earth shall rise to praise your name and dwell forever in your peace. Amen.

2nd Lent, Year B
Genesis 17:1–10
Mark 8:31–38

4.
God of tenderness and strength, under the shelter of your wings the night harbors no terrors, only peaceful stars bearing promise. We praise you for giving refuge and for pointing us toward the

stars. In peace we rest in your presence; in strength we go forth into the world. Amen.

> 2nd Lent, Year C
> Genesis 15:1–12
> Luke 13:31–35

5.

We praise you, God,
for summoning the morning sun to banish darkness;
for wresting peace out of despair;
for restoring hope to the brokenhearted.
You brood over the abyss of our darkness
until we are raised by your presence to life renewed.
We praise you, O God, for love eternal,
love more gracious than the coming of spring. Amen.

> 4th Lent, Year B
> John 3:14–21

6.

O Lord, Giver of Bread, many times we have tasted your kindness and found you to be good to all your children. When, like Israel's children, we walked the ungiving desert, your provisions sustained us daily. When, like the prodigal, we were brought to our senses by hunger and need, you awaited our return with feasting and joy. You, O God, are the nourishing presence giving refuge to all who seek your love. For mercy poured out like manna, we praise you and thank you, O Lord, Giver of Bread. Amen.

> 4th Lent, Year C
> Psalm 34:1–8
> Joshua 5:9–12
> Luke 15:1–3, 11–32

7.

O God, the only source of life, in the beginning your breath and Spirit drew forth the world until the earth was filled with your creatures. At the last your breath shall gather us in, each in our time, to the shelter and mystery of your love. We praise you, God, for the certainty that in death, as in life, we are sustained by your love. Amen.

> 5th Lent, Year B
> John 12:20–23

8.

O Jesus our Redeemer, like the pilgrims of old Jerusalem, we are stirred by your presence. In you, gentle Savior, we see God on earth. Walk in our midst this hour, to awaken our hearts and nourish our souls. Increase in us that strength which is manifested in humble service. Amen.

> Palm Sunday, Year A
> Matthew 21:1–11

9.

God of Mercy, we can scarcely perceive the extravagance of your holy love for all generations. In Jesus our Christ, you entered into the beauty and the anguish of our lives. Jesus poured out his spirit in compassion that we might come to know the splendid fullness of your divine care. On this day when Jesus deliberately enters our lives, grant us the wisdom to proclaim his praise with sincerity and love, lavish in response to his self-giving. Grant us endurance to persevere in faith when the acclaim has ceased and darkness falls upon the city. Amen.

> Passion Sunday/Palm Sunday, Year B
> Mark 11:1–11
> (Mark 14:1–11)
> Philippians 2:5–11

10.

Holy God, if we were mute in the face of mystery,
silent before beauty and wonder,
the dust beneath our feet would sing
and stones tremble with the melody of praise!
You have shed light over all creation;
earth and all creatures are resplendent in your love.
We praise you for giving us entrance
into the everlasting Light!
May we be found constant in devotion
even as jubilation turns to lament,
willing even in sorrow to cry out in steadfast faith
to you, our God. Amen.

> Palm Sunday, Year C
> Psalm 118:19–29
> Luke 19:28–40

11.

Christ our Shepherd, in the evening shadows you are surrounded by death and stalked by the enemy. Yet even in the valley of death, you offer us the cup of plenty and would feast us with life. Jesus, loving Shepherd, help us to trust and to follow you. Grant that we may not scatter when you are seized, but help us to abide with you through the great darkness to the dawn that will surely come. Amen.

Maundy Thursday
(Psalm 23)
(Hosea 6:3)
(Mark 14:27)

12.

O Living Christ, this evening as we gather for prayer we are reminded of your solitary vigil in the garden. It must have been hard to break bread with your disciples that night, knowing that later one would betray you; one deny you; and all sleep out of weariness and hopelessness, when you needed them most. With you, O Christ, we pray that the cup of testing be removed from us. We pray that God's will be worked in our lives. Preserve us from the Gethsemane sleep and the sorrow of those who live without hope. Keep us vigilant in prayer, steadfast in trust, and grateful for your risen presence. Amen.

Maundy Thursday

13.

Eternal God, you neither slumber nor sleep in your watchful care for all creation. The knowledge of your vigilant protection gives us comfort and confidence. You hold us in strong arms. You sustain us through every hardship and sorrow. We trust that with you upholding us no fantasy of our dark hours and no creature of the shadows shall ever undo us. You are the Light in darkness, and in your presence is perfect tranquillity.

We do not ask to be delivered from every conflict or hardship, but we ask to be awakened from our sleep, from our sheltered faith. Give us the gift of watchfulness, that we might recognize Christ within each person and see clearly what you would have us do. Grant us such vigilance that we might desert neither Jesus nor you when you call upon us with some ministry to perform. This we pray through Christ who walks beside us and bids us watch. Amen.

Maundy Thursday
(Psalm 121:3–4)
(Mark 14:26–50)
(John 1:5)

PRAYERS OF CONFESSION

1.

We confess, O God, that though you have borne us through barren
deserts we remain unchanged. We erase the tracks of our pilgrimage and blot out the memory of our trials. As your angels ministered to Jesus in the wilderness, you have also sustained us. But
we have forgotten your providence. Jesus emerged from the wilderness afire, urgently proclaiming your presence, but we have
emerged with indifference to your demands. God have mercy
upon us, who are complacent in the face of divine miracle and
divine demand. Amen.

> 1st Lent, Year B
> Mark 1:9–15

2.

Call to Confession: God's faithful have never found their journey
comfortable. Noah faced torrential waters; Abraham and Sarah
were called to leave their home; the Hebrews' exodus led into the
desert; and Jesus was led by the Spirit into fields of desolation. But
we cannot tolerate any deviation from our plans, even if it is God
who calls us into uncertainty. Let us confess our sin.

We confess, O God, that we cannot follow Jesus on his wilderness
journey to seek your will. We cannot come before you without
buffers lessening the impact of your demand and the hardship it
might entail. We require our routines, our comforts and our plans.
As we organize our lives, we schedule our time with you into
comfortable parcels of time, calculated emotion, and preplanned
responses of giving and service. Have mercy upon us, O God.
Forgive us for failing to follow you. Free us for the love that trusts
you no matter where you lead or how rough the path may be.
Amen.

> 1st Lent, Year C
> Luke 4:1–13

3.

O Christ, we share the strengths and the frailties of your first
disciples. We share their devotion to you. We share their weaknesses: we do not fully trust in your power to heal and to save. Nor
do we believe that we share in these gifts. We find your words
cloaked in riddle and parable, your actions hard to understand.
Like Peter, we refuse to believe that rejection, sacrifice, and death

can ever be God's way. Yet, O Jesus, you love us and continually call us to your side. Cleanse our hearts of selfishness and fear; give us the love that bears all things, believes all things, and hopes and endures all things. Amen.

2nd Lent, Year B
Mark 8:31–38
(1 Corinthians 13:7)

4.

LEADER: O God, we do not trust you enough to simply rest in your love, like Abraham, silently numbering the stars and hearing your promise.

PEOPLE: We have stubbornly refused invitations to await your leisure.

LEADER: Even now Christ would gather us as a hen gathers her brood,

PEOPLE: Yet we fear intimacy with love and reject the refuge of his love.

LEADER: Forgive us, O God.

PEOPLE: Teach us that unless we trustingly rest in your love,

LEADER: We cannot claim the power to serve you.

ALL: Forgive us and give us your peace. Amen.

2nd Lent, Year C
Genesis 15:1–12
Luke 13:31–35

5.

Call to Confession: Holy ground and holy places are not hidden on high mountains or in distant countries. Holy ground lies beneath our feet. In our brokenness we fail to realize the sacredness of familiar places and people. Let us confess our sin.

God of Moses, you call us as you called the faithful of ancient times—mysteriously shedding light in the midst of uneventful days. Through a shrub alight with divine fire, you reveal that our common days are steeped in holiness and mystery. We confess that we fail to recognize that all ground is holy ground, or that our routine lives are encompassed by splendor, or that this day is the time when you call us to do your work. Forgive us, God. Free us to see the blessing of your presence, and give us the strength to work as you call us. Amen.

3rd Lent, Year C
Exodus 3:1–15

6.

O God, we confess that our experiences of suffering make us doubt your promise and power. Like those captive in Babylon, we see no reason and no way to sing your praise. In the depth of our darkness, we do not see your Light. In our isolation, we do not feel your nearness. Forgive us, God. For you gave up your own Son for us, and never promised a world without suffering, but that you would bear us through it. Cleanse us of all bitterness and doubt, and renew us in your merciful Spirit. Amen.

> 4th Lent, Year B
> Psalm 137:1–6
> John 3:14–21

7.

Call to Confession: Friends, we may not claim the grand, obvious sins of the prodigal, but like the elder brother, we have all made transgressions that quelled the flow of God's love through us. Let us confess our sin.

O God, we don't have much to confess. For we are not so much prodigal sons and daughters who have squandered a fortune as we are elder sons and daughters, dutiful, faithful, and true. But God, we are perplexed by the extravagance of your mercy, surpassing every human standard of fairness. We are resentful and angered by your goodness to those who always need to be bailed out of trouble. We confess not deeds of mischief, but the dangerous feelings of resentment, jealousy, and the refusal to forgive and feel joy. God, forgive our invisible caustic sins. Free us to love generously, without calculation. Amen.

> 4th Lent, Year C
> Luke 15:1–3, 11–32

8.

Call to Confession: Our lives are embraced by mystery at birth, at death, and through all our years. We have not trusted that the mystery points to the presence of God. Let us confess our sin.

Christ our Lord, you have told us that life is gained by losing it, giving it away, and letting it go in death. We confess that these words frighten us, for we give it up unwillingly. Christ, your entire life was immersed in holy mystery. But we keep mystery at bay, never relinquishing our control of events or pausing to consider the Spirit's direction. Jesus, you taught that we must die to yield a harvest of life. Teach us what it means to let go, that we might be embraced by divine love, forever beyond our control and bidding, forever bountiful in mercy. Amen.

5th Lent, Year B
John 12:20–33

9.

Jesus, divine Companion, at Bethany among your dear friends we see your tender side: weeping because of Mary's grief, sharing meals with loved ones, accepting the outpouring of love's tenderness. It scarcely occurs to us that you, solace for our despair, should yourself need the wordless balm of tenderness. If we have ignored your human needs for kindness, how much more have we run roughshod over our friends and family and those we call strangers? Like Judas we resent generous outpourings of love when the energy and wealth they represent could be used for more tangible purposes. Help us realize, Jesus, that if we do not love and care for each other, our lives are barren and harsh. Forgive us, and free us like Mary for spontaneous affection for each other and you. Amen.

5th Lent, Year C
John 12:1–8

10.

Christ our Lord, you have graced our lives with a love lavish beyond measure. Emptied of any selfish ambition, you poured yourself out for us with a resolution that shames our pale commitments. The depth and breadth of your love should inspire us to a ministry knowing no barriers and no limits in its kindness. Our response has hardly been as generous. We are timid in love and reserved in affection. We squelch our impulses to recklessly show our love for others. And our love for you, far from being wholehearted, is undermined by fickle enthusiasms and devious desires. Christ our Savior, have mercy upon us. Cleanse our hearts. And through your loving Spirit, empower us to love as you have loved us. Amen.

Passion Sunday/Palm Sunday, Year B
(Mark 14:1–11)
Mark 11:1–11
Philippians 2:5–11

11.

Call to Confession: Everyone loves a parade. But the Palm Sunday procession led by Jesus is not a lighthearted parade. It is his proclamation: "I am in your midst as Messiah. Accept the love of God!" We watch as fickle bystanders or hardened Pharisees. Let us confess our sin.

Merciful God, we confess that we are embarrassed by those who noisily acclaim Christ as Lord. Like the Pharisees, we would like to see jubilance restrained and feeling expressed in quiet moderation. Have mercy upon us, God. If we fail to express joy in our Savior, the very earth will resound in praise! We confess how quickly we rally around those whose fervent prayer is "Give me success," but how quick we are to desert the suffering whose prayer is "Not my will, but yours." Have mercy upon us, God, fair-weather followers of Jesus Christ. Amen.

> Palm Sunday, Year C
> Psalm 118:25
> Luke 19:28–40
> (Luke 22:42)

Assurance of Pardon: The inestimable mercy of God is not diminished by the wavering strength of our faith nor by our capacity for joy. The mercy of God is poured upon us, faithful and faithless, joyful and joyless alike, that all may come to know the boundless love of God. Friends, simply accept the good news: In Jesus Christ you are forgiven. Amen.

12.
Call to Confession: Christ, the Bread of Life and the True Vine, offers us the gifts that nourish the soul. In our brokenness we have spurned his love, which could amply supply our need. Let us confess our sin.

O Lord, Giver of Bread, how often you would strengthen us with your presence! Daily you offer the refreshment of your love. Daily you would empower us to live as faithful servants. We confess that we have not sought your company. We have doubted that you can satisfy the hungers that plague us. And we are frightened to think what changes your presence might work in our lives. Forgive us, Lord, our failure to trust you. Give us courage to accept your provisions. For, no less than you asked your disciples, you ask us to endure, to watch, and to pray with you at your hour of trial. Amen.

> Maundy Thursday, Year B
> Mark 14:12–26

Assurance of Pardon: Jesus our Christ has come to a world of sorrow and sin, of sickness and death. He comes to us who need him. He has borne our burdens; he has carried our sorrows. In his broken body he broke sin and death. Believe and rejoice in what he has accomplished: by his wounds we have been healed, and death no longer has dominion. Praise be to God! Amen.

Good Friday A,B,C
Isaiah 53:4–5, 12
(Romans 6:9)

PASTORAL PRAYERS

1.

O God, Keeper of the Promise, as you guided Noah over flood-waters, so you sustain our ark, the earth, and its inhabitants through every travail. To strengthen us for endurance, you send the dove bearing hope, and the rainbow promising your hallowed peace. Bear us all, who live on this fragile vessel, over the waves of conflict that assail us. Like Noah, his family, and all the animals, we find that life adrift in the ark demands endurance and patience. For the raven of despair returns to us, announcing that the floodwaters of destruction yet cover the earth, and we feel helpless to bid them diminish. O Lord our God, strengthen us to trust in your promise of peace. Strengthen us to bear up our side of the covenant, stemming the tides of war and violence. As rivers gain force from each drop of water, so violence is fed by every flaring temper, each abusive action and word, every hurt ignored, and every gun that is fired. O God, strengthen us to banish violence, and to pray and work for the peace of the world, our home, and your dwelling place.

1st Lent, Year B
Genesis 9:8–17

2.

God of power and mystery, just as Abraham and Sarah were taken by surprise with your blessing so late in life, and Jesus was confronted with the cross in his prime, so we do not know when on our journey your purpose and power will interrupt and redirect our own intentions. If you surprise us with unexpected happiness, grant us the grace to fully embrace it. If you call us to a season of suffering, grant us the wisdom to see that this too may be your hand. As you redeemed Jesus' wretched death on the cross, you shall also work through our trials for blessing and love. Help us, with Jesus, to will your will and to walk in your presence, all the days of our lives.

> 2nd Lent, Year B
> (Genesis 16:15–17)
> Genesis 17:1–10, 15–19
> Mark 8:31–38

3.

God, you are the only hope of the exiled and homeless. Through the strength you have given us, we are resilient in adversity, trouble, and defeat. We thank you for the hope you supply when we think we are defeated and for the endurance you supply when we are past effort and caring. Much of our strength is rooted in this place, our home. We see the world through contented eyes and cannot fathom how those forced to leave their homes can cope with their problems. Open our eyes to the plight of the exile. Help us to understand the wariness, the fears and resentment that exile enforces—and so increase in us the compassion to offer shelter in Jesus' name. As your Son roamed the countryside that he might dwell in each person's heart, we pray for your presence and help for all those exiled from their homes.

> 4th Lent, Year B
> Psalm 137:1–7

4.

Holy God, the majesty of your ways far surpasses our richest imagining. Your forgiveness is so complete that its graciousness leaves us baffled. Your love is so pure that ours seems grudging in comparison. In the light of your splendor, we stand revealed as but pale, imperfect reflections of your image. O God, have mercy upon us, who can scarcely comprehend how vast your love is. God, you welcome us to your side, beyond our deserving. You daily give us bread that satisfies our hunger. You forgive us far beyond human standards of forgiveness. Teach us that there is no virtue in the jealous calculations of the elder son, even if we have borne our duties without complaint. If we do not love and cannot celebrate a sinner's reform and return, we are lost ourselves. Teach us elder sons and daughters the sweet joy of forgiveness.

> 4th Lent, Year C
> Luke 15:1–3, 11–32

5.

Lord, we know that if we try to live as you lived, we too shall be condemned. It is much easier to live by simply reacting to people rather than responding to them with the love which first asks, "What is God's will?" The world becomes suspicious of our intentions when we pause not to figure our own advantage, but to figure what is to the advantage of God. Yet, Lord, we know that you are right. Help us to live your gospel. Help us to speak and respond in love, wherever you lead us. To follow daily where you call is to carry the cross.

6.

Most merciful God, in the gift of your Son you have hallowed our lives and drawn us close to yourself. Nothing that can happen to us lies outside the scope of your caring for us. You are close to sustain and teach us at all times. Yet we do not see the hallowedness of the earth and the mystery enveloping us at every turn. Jesus has told us that divine presence is as enmeshed in our lives as yeast in bread, as fruitful in our lives as the great bush grown from a tiny mustard seed. Even events such as death, which seem to signal God's absence, shall with your love yield a harvest of the Spirit. God, open our eyes to the tantalizing richness and sacred love with which you uphold all creation. Help us to truly trust Jesus' word that as his death was fruitful for the life of the world, he can redeem all hopeless situations in our lives as well.

5th Lent, Year B
John 12:20–33

7.

Christ our Savior, the beauty of your life and love graces us like the fragrance of spring flowers. As the hyacinth and the lily are reckless in beauty, so you have spared no effort to bring graciousness to our lives. One woman recognized you as the source of beauty and bathed you with perfume. But unlike her, we have been blind to the graciousness of your life. We have not responded to you with lavish devotion.

Forgive us, Lord. We have not recognized the beauty of your love. Even less have we recognized the bracing reality of your message: that the humble shall be exalted, the first last; that if we die with you, we shall live with you. Sacrificial love is foreign to us. We have scarcely an idea of the compassion which loves without restraint and self-centeredness. And though you have called us friends, we berate ourselves too consistently to take your invitation with the seriousness it deserves. We feel unworthy to share the life that you offer. Forgive us, Lord. O Christ, you are the Resurrection and the Life. Through your Spirit you can transform us and help us accept the life that you offer. During the coming week of trial, anguish, and death, teach us sacrifice and self-giving; teach us trust in God's ultimate affirmation; and gently help us to die to all in our lives that does not show forth your love.

Passion Sunday, Year B
Mark 14:1–11
Philippians 2:5–11

8.

O Gentle Savior, you declared God to be present to us in a gracious and festive way. If we find it nearly impossible to stand by the cross in your hour of anguish, it is because we, like you, cannot comprehend that such a gracious God would abandon you, offering no comfort in your affliction, speaking no words in the deadening silence, refusing to intervene in your suffering and torment. This is the cup of suffering that you long dreaded. Yet you did not seek to ease the pain—refusing the wine mixed with myrrh. You did not curse your executioners. You bore the derision, the scourging, and the crucifixion, calling from the depths of your horror, calling to the last upon your God.

Christ, you have been delivered up to cross and nail, delivered up to death and sealed behind the final stone. All this you bore for us, suffering and dying that we might be born to eternal life. O Lord, be with us in every hour of darkness and torment. Help us to endure any hours of tortured questioning of God. Teach us what it means to die to self that the unfathomable purposes of God may break through in some unforeseeable dawn. Remembering your suffering and with the quiet trust that God raised you from death, we pray with you the prayer you have given disciples of all generations: Our Father . . .

Passion Sunday, Year B
Mark 15:1–39

9.

God in whom the heart's deep terrors are assuaged and the furrowed brow soothed to long-sought peace, hear our prayers for all whose darkest night still lies before them. No more than Christ are we exempt from deepest distress; no less than he are we granted the deep delight of your presence, when darkness yields to the great morning light. Hold tenderly in your arms all who are weary, embattled, and shattered, until, strength spent, they become empty, open vessels to your Spirit. Then you will restore them, as surely as Christ rose from the tomb into everlasting light. Amen.

Passion Sunday A,B,C
Psalm 31:9–16
(Philippians 2:5–11)

EASTER

CALLS TO WORSHIP

1.

LEADER: This is the day which the Lord has made. Let us rejoice and be glad in it!

PEOPLE: This is the day that the stone is cast aside and the mantle of darkness is cast away!

LEADER: God has swallowed up death forever and brushed the tears from our faces.

PEOPLE: This is the day of salvation.

LEADER: Be glad and rejoice—the Lord of Light has come and reigns forever. Christ is risen!

PEOPLE: He is risen indeed!

ALL: Alleluia! Amen.

> Easter, Year B
> Isaiah 25:6–9
> Psalm 118:24 (27)

2.

LEADER: When death has broken our spirit, we wake prepared for grief and sorrow.

PEOPLE: Joy is foreign and resurrection is an idle dream.

LEADER: But hope dawned long ago—the morning of the new creation!

PEOPLE: The myrrh-bearing women, prepared for mourning, were called to joy instead!

LEADER: May their witness give you hope.

PEOPLE: This is the third day. The tomb is empty, our cherished dream fulfilled!

LEADER: Christ is risen!

PEOPLE: He is risen indeed!

ALL: Thanks be to God! Amen.

> Easter, Year C
> Luke 24:1–12

3.

Jesus has passed through the door of death and opened the way to the blessing of life. As on the third day, his presence can penetrate the barrier of our fears and give us peace, that we may proclaim the beauty of forgiveness and the strength that community supplies. Friends, Christ is risen and he is here. Let us worship God, who blesses us with life.

2nd Easter, Year B
John 20:19–31
Psalm 133:3

4.

Friends, Christ draws close to us. His presence is not announced so much by searing light or angelic song, as it is by the gradual recognition of something holy enmeshed in our daily lives: simple as salt, common as bread, as unexpected as a treasure buried in a field! Such is the presence of Christ with us in each ordinary day. Let us praise God with joy!

3rd Easter, Year A
Luke 24:13–35
(Matthew 13:44–46)

5.

People of God, because Jesus conquered death, we can live! To the disciples Jesus was not merely a memory or an apparition. He was present, guiding them in their daily tasks, kindling a fire, serving breakfast. Christ is also present to us, close to hear and answer prayer, to guide us, to encourage the wise use of gifts. Confident that Christ is risen and present, and thankful for the gift of new life, let us worship God together!

3rd Easter, Year C
John 21:1–19

6.

Friends, the Good Shepherd calls.
Listen to his voice and follow him.
He will lead you beside waters of rest;
He will restore your souls;
He will show you the paths of justice.
With joy let us praise the God of
shepherding care!

4th Easter, Year B
Psalm 23
John 10:22–30

7.

Come to Christ, people of God, taste the kindness of the Lord! He gives you every provision and fills you with good things. Come to Christ, you chosen people, and be built upon the cornerstone into a spiritual home where all may find rest for the evening and courage and strength for the day. With joy let us give praise to God!

> 5th Easter, Year A
> (Psalm 107:9)
> 1 Peter 2:2–10

8.

LEADER: Jesus said, "I am the vine and my Father is the vine-dresser.

PEOPLE: "Abide in me, and I in you. I am the vine, you are the branches.

LEADER: "Those who abide in me shall bear much fruit.

PEOPLE: "If you abide in me, ask whatever you will, and it shall be done for you.

LEADER: "These things I have spoken to you, that your joy may be full."

ALL: Trusting the promises of our Lord, we rejoice in his presence and we worship with joy!

> 5th Easter, Year B
> John 15:1–8 (9–11), adapted

9.

Friends, you are chosen by Christ; you are those he calls friends, and asks to share his labor. As he was unrecognized on the road by his disciples, so he draws near to us in hidden presence. Let us worship him who has called and blessed us. Let us give God praise!

> 6th Easter, Year B
> John 15:9–17

10.

As earth yields its increase of beauty and the promise of fruit to come, so God supplies grace without measure: with light and peace, God dawns in the hearts of the faithful. Let us worship God, giver of peace. Amen.

> 6th Easter, Year C
> Psalm 67
> John 14:23–29

PRAYERS OF PRAISE

1.
God most holy, like a bright morning star Christ has risen. All sorrow and darkness flee in his presence. He is not captive in the stone tomb, but alive. And we find him in our midst where he has always been. Christ the Good Shepherd laid down his life for us, giving us life overflowing with richness and mercy. He gathers us into one flock, yet cares for us individually, calling us each by name. O God, we praise you for the Good Shepherd, who seeks us out, abides in our midst, and gives us eternal life. Amen.

Easter A,B,C
John 20:1–18

2.
O Risen Christ, you go before us and have always gone before us. Born as an infant, you assumed all our helplessness. Growing as a child into adulthood, you endured the trials and enjoyed the joys of our lives. Living and working in Galilee, you learned the frustrations and the boundless hungers of human life, the temptations that entice us, and the splendors in which we find our lives hallowed and graced. Christ, you have gone before us into death, and have risen to stand before us in splendor! We thank you and praise you, Gentle Savior, for love that is one with us in compassion; for love that goes before us, opening the way of light and mercy; for love that stands before us, pointing the way, directing our steps and summoning us to follow. Amen.

Easter, Year B
Mark 16:1–8

3.
Living Spirit, when all was dark and deep, there was only the breath of God hovering upon the waters. But the breath was sufficient to bring the blessing of life to earth. Now, O Living Spirit, you are sufficient to bring life to us, wresting peace and devotion from lonely, fearful hearts. O Spirit, we praise you for the blessing that overtakes us unaware, for the peace that dawns each day, and the work for which you empower us. Amen.

2nd Easter A,B,C
John 20:19–31
(Genesis 1:1–2; 2:7)

4.

God of all creatures, this morning we are intoxicated by the sweetness of spring, exhilarated by the exuberance of plants: everything that sends down roots, reveals buds, and stretches to the light. God, turn our attention gently to the growth stirring within us, to a presence not as captivating to our senses as it is infinitely precious to our hearts. Christ no longer agonizes in the garden, is no longer fixed upon the cross, no longer lies within the tomb. He is risen, walking the roads that we walk, facing our life shoulder to shoulder with us. Grant us the eyes of faith and trusting hearts, O God, to see our Risen Lord and to hear what he bids us do. Amen.

3rd Easter, Year A
Luke 24:13–35

5.

O God, like fishers who toil all night in vain over a sea brimming with fish, sometimes we live unaware of joy, possibility, and blessing. The abundant harvest eludes our grasp. In this hour help us to recognize Jesus' presence, to accept his gifts, and to join him in service. Amen.

3rd Easter, Year C
John 21:1–19

6.

O Shepherd God, you have blessed us with peace as tranquil as a flowing stream; peace that nourishes as food and sleep; peace that is stronger than death. You call us to rest in your care that we may live with courage. Though fears beset us, your love will comfort us again. Though death is no stranger, you shall be our last and best friend. We thank you, Shepherd God, for your love that fills us to overflowing, this day and forever. Amen.

4th Easter A,B,C
Psalm 23

7.

O God, all seasons are seasons of your mercy. Seedtime or harvest, winter barrenness or summer plenitude, all are alike to you: any season is the time to sow new seed; any season is the time to rest from labor; all seasons are occasions to bring your people to an ample harvest of the Spirit. We thank you, God, for perennial mercies, lavish in response to our continual need. Amen.

> 5th Easter, Year B
> John 15:1–8

8.
In the flush of new-sprung life the earth yields its treasures, every new blade of grass, sculpted flower, and budding tree exults, "Our lives continue, praise be to God!" Let all who have breath praise God, who delivers us from desolation and gives us the everlasting jubilant season! Amen.

> 6th Easter, Year C
> Psalm 67:6

9.
Most Holy God, your Spirit dwells within us as vital and deep as the beating of the heart, as steady as the drawing of breath. You raise within each of us an interior song of unutterable joy and unfading hope. Sound through our lives now and forever. Bless and uphold us, that through the channel of our lives the whole body of Christ may be blessed and healed. Amen.

10.
O Christ our Lord, in light and splendor you are exalted over the earth, that you may reign in the hearts of all people. You bear love never to be eclipsed, whose brilliance illumines and empowers us. You are the life of the world, life-giver to all. In wonder and joy we cry "Alleluia!" Amen.

> Ascension A,B,C
> Acts 1:1–11

11.
O God, like a mother embracing her child, you hold us close to your heart. Your love shelters and protects, feeds our great hunger, releases us into the world, yet always watches over us, prays for us, and longs to see the promise of our lives fulfilled. We thank you for all mothers whose care for their children reflects your divine care for us. Hold us close to your great heart, O God, that we may fully know the peace and strength that flow from your presence. Amen.

PRAYERS OF AFFIRMATION

1.
God of love, we gather to praise you and declare your mercy! In days of despair we had scattered, each to our mourning. But you have gathered us to feast us with joy. We were buried in despair, lifeless, without hope. But you have raised us, proclaiming love stronger than death. As surely as the rising sun banishes the shadows of night, Christ's resurrection gives the world love undimmed by any force of darkness. Christ is here and he goes before us! In his presence we find our deliverance and our direction: for he gives to us, as to all the disciples, a new beginning and a holy work to do. Amen.

> Easter, Year B
> Mark 16:1–8
> Isaiah 25:6–9
> (Song of Solomon 8:6–7)

2.
O Jesus our Redeemer, we thank you that our fears and sorrows are no barrier to your love. Whenever we have retreated behind closed doors, you have sought us out to comfort and strengthen us. Though we have not felt the breath of your presence like the disciples, yet we have felt you close to us. Each time a fresh peace dispels anxiety, each time we feel the impulse to serve another in love, we have signs of your closeness to us. We thank you for calling us to share in your work of love and justice, and for the sense of communion we find in your church. Draw near to all who live in fear; refresh all who are dispirited; restore the lonely to the joy of friendship; and send us to share in this ministry and to help fulfill these prayers. Amen.

> 2nd Easter A,B,C
> John 20:19–31

3.
God, we are just ordinary people leading ordinary lives. For the most part, our lives are like a garment that is drab in color, dull in shape, and flat in texture. Just as we think we cannot bear one more boring day, something wondrous happens: we begin to see that our lives are indeed hallowed by your invigorating presence. We remember that Christ revealed your love through the most ordinary of things: salt, light, bread, flowers, and common, even inconspicuous, people. He wants to draw close to us as we go

about our routine tasks, lifting our eyes to the splendor of creation. God, open our hearts to the mystery and grace about us. And let Christ be known to us in gestures as simple as the breaking of bread. Amen.

3rd Easter, Year A
Luke 24:13–35

4.

Holy God, we thank you for your shepherding care. When we are consumed with longing and envy, you grant us the contentment that comes from the peace of your presence. When we are beset by fear and harried by enemies, you grant us shelter and restore tranquillity. Always vigilant, you have rescued us from danger we could not foresee or prevent. And if we were hurt, you have tended us as a mother soothes her wounded child. Wherever we venture and whatever hardship we encounter, we rejoice that we can always trust in your presence to help us endure. No enemy, no evil, not even death itself can separate us from the love which you pour upon us. Loving God, open our hearts to receive the bounty of your blessing; and, having quenched our need, send us to shepherd all those in need of your care. Amen.

4th Easter A,B,C
Psalm 23
(Isaiah 66:13)

5.

O God, as a gardener who loves and needs the fruit of the garden, you tend us that we may grow and flourish. You have planted the seeds of love and justice within us, and are joyful when we bring your long efforts to fruition. There are times when you must prune us, that we may direct our energies into more fruitful channels We thank you for caring to direct and discipline our otherwise haphazard efforts. Like any gardener who loves to survey growing crops and branches bearing buds, you, O God, kneel beside us, rejoicing when we grow, suffering when we are set back. You have made our very lives the field from which you will draw a rich harvest. Thank you, God, for abiding in our midst and tending us. May we call to mind often the continual flow of your Spirit through us, which gives us life. May we never do anything to sever that vital connection. As you help us to be branches bearing fruit, so use us to cultivate the fruit of the Spirit in each other. Amen.

5th Easter, Year B
Johr 15:1–8

6.

God of tender mercy, in your Spirit all the earth's children find welcome, shelter, and peace. Even if we journey to the far ends of the earth, we find your Spirit embracing us, offering a home of compassion and rest. We thank you for the Spirit, who brings to remembrance the words of Jesus our Lord; who leads us to recall your acts of mercy when we are in distress; who teaches us and guides us as surely as if Christ were beside us in the flesh. Like a wise and loving friend, we know that with your affirmation we may always dwell secure. You hallow all the earth and all moments, O God, making all time and space our home as well. Thank you for permeating our world, so that we may trust and believe in your love. Amen.

> 6th Easter, Year C
> Psalm 67
> John 14:23–29

7.

O Christ, you have ascended into the realm of everlasting light. Yet you are not distant from us. The fullness of your Spirit enfolds us like the warmth of the summer sun, bathing us with light, enabling us to flourish. As you bade the sick rise from their knees in Galilee, you call us to ascend into the peace of your presence. As you sent out the disciples, you direct us to serve with love and joy. We praise you, O Christ, for you have shown us that God's immeasurable power is at work in our lives as in the whole of creation. Amen.

> Ascension A,B,C
> Mark 16:9–16, 19–20
> Ephesians 1:15–23

PASTORAL PRAYERS

1.

Marvelous God, in your bountiful love, by the breath of your Spirit, you created the world and all that lives within it. By your mercy you re-create both the earth and our hearts after every winter season. We praise you for continually transforming us to reflect that first splendid day of creation. Because you love all creatures and the stirring of new life, humanity has always met you in gardens. You placed Adam and Eve in the bountiful garden of paradise, where you fed them. But when you came to share the beauty with them, they hid from you. So too, we shrink from fully accepting your gracious care. Have mercy upon us who cannot yet fully affirm that you give us Eden as our dwelling. With Jesus and the disciples, we have lived in the garden of Gethsemane, the garden of trial. There in sorrow we sought your presence, yet received only the answer of silence. Our friends fell away, and, fearing abandonment by you as well, we plummeted to the depths of sorrow. But, God, your plan of providence continues in the garden of the resurrection. There, when we least expect it, we hear your gentle voice and know that you are near. This time we don't run to hide as Adam and Eve did. For suffering has taught us to embrace your love. We hear your voice; we accept your love. In joy we declare your risen presence and gift of life to all. O God, you come to meet us in the garden, sharing the beauty and the bounty of life. Root us forever in the one who is the true vine and only ground of mercy, that we may be filled with all the fullness of your Spirit and power, forever and ever.

Easter A,B,C
John 20:1–18

2.

Risen Savior, true to your promise, you go before us. And we see you, as did those to whom you ministered in Galilee. We see your presence wherever the troubled are calmed and the wounded healed, wherever people are fed and clothed, whenever the lost are gathered back to your side. We praise you, O Christ, that having risen, you live in our midst, still healing, teaching, and summoning men and women to loving service. O Lord, you have kept your promise of presence despite the power of evil and death. Your Word has emerged unscathed from the crucible of death. Thus we know the trustworthiness of all divine promise. God's love endures forever; we shall be gathered to your side in the realm of endless light and life. We praise you, O Savior, for love stronger than death.

God, as the women mourned and trembled with fear the very morning that Christ rose from the grave, there are many who live with brokenness, sadness, and tragedy, despite the presence of the Risen Christ. We pray for all who mourn and are troubled, all whose lives are sundered by forces beyond their control. Open their eyes and hearts to your healing presence and send us, we pray, to heal, comfort, and work, for the world needs us.

Easter, Year B
Mark 16:1–8
(Song of Solomon 8:6)

3.

Living God, through Christ a precious treasure has been delivered
to us. It is a living, vibrant hope, more precious than gold, more
sturdy than diamonds, more enduring than any gem. It is imper-
ishable, unfading, the pearl of great price. Such is the treasure of
your love for us. This gift does not exempt us from muddying our
hands in fields of labor. It does not exempt us from hardship, loss,
or tragedy. Instead, this precious gift is given in the midst of these,
and is strengthened by them. If our faith is tested, it emerges
refined: stronger and more compassionate. Grant us, God, that we
might value this treasure of relationship with you. Let the Risen
Christ go before us, calling and challenging us. Let him be behind
us, for protection. And let him be beside us, as one who knows our
struggles, our temptations, and our hopes. Strengthen and steady
us in prayer; widen our hearts' compassion; open and use our
hands for service. And in all things, come to us with your presence, for in your love lies deep, unutterable, and exalted joy!

2nd Easter, Year A
1 Peter 1:3–9

4.

O God, you bless us with life. We thank you for the presence of
the Risen Christ. No barrier that we erect can obstruct Christ's
power to find and heal us. No doubts that we harbor can change
Christ's willingness to bless and call us. Christ has placed the open
door of mercy before us, and comes to us whenever we linger
behind doors locked by fear. God, we thank you for all your
witnesses to the Risen Christ—for Mary Magdalene, for all the
disciples and followers who cared for us, centuries distant, and
recorded the Easter event that we might have joy, believing in his
presence. Though we have not touched Jesus or seen him as they
did, his spirit graces us as fully as it did those early followers, who,
in their joy and empowered by the Spirit, lived together in the
community that led to the church. We are heirs of their witness,
belief, and joy, as we are heirs of your grace. We thank you, God,
for the Risen Christ and for the church.

2nd Easter, Year B
Psalm 133:3
John 20:19–31

5.

O Jesus, risen in splendor and splendid in power, abide with us, for the evening comes. Hallow our hearts with your light and peace. Jesus, bless our lives; let us shine with the luster of stars. From this fragile clay, mold an inestimable treasure! Jesus, bless our lives, draw near to us and others. Teach us how close God is, how deeply we are loved. Let the simplest things convey splendor, truth, and summons. O Jesus, risen in splendor and splendid in power, abide with us, for the evening comes. Abide with us, and grant the world your peace.

3rd Easter, Year A
Luke 24:13–35
(2 Corinthians 4:7)

6.

Most loving God, keep us true to our promise to love each other and to love you. For nothing is easier than to love merely in our words and the inner speech of our prayers. Help us to love in deeds that are as visible as Jesus' acts of compassion.

We ask forgiveness when we lose courage and leave the sorrowing without comfort, the fearful without hope, victims of any trouble without aid. Though we scarcely deserve your mercy for our failure of love, we ask you to help us in these times, that your love may empower and restore us to a love that is forthright and passionately concerned for all your creatures.

Impress upon our hearts, O God, the truth that nothing is so urgently needed in our world as love in action, and nothing so deeply desired as the shelter of your peace. God, keep us faithful to our promise to love, as you fulfill all your promises.

4th Easter, Year B
1 John 3:18–24

7.

Loving God, you tend us as carefully as a farmer laboring over the fields and as lovingly as a gardener cultivating flowers. We thank you for the nourishment we receive from your hand, for the guidance that you provide in our growth, for the fruitfulness that you expect from us, which motivates us to grow in all grace. Deliver us from the pride that would give us the illusion of self-sufficiency. For we can do nothing without your love flowing through us and the opportunity to pass your love on to others. Deliver us from the self-pity in which we deem ourselves inadequate to bear fruit for you. For with your care, each of us can be brought to fruition; none are dispensable. God, work through our lives that we may bear all the fruits of mercy. Help us always to abide in your Spirit, and use each of us to share in the labor of the harvest.

5th Easter, Year B
John 15:1–8

8.

Everlasting God, the span of our life, though it may stretch for long years ahead of us, is brief, a mere candle flame burning to the edge of the taper, when compared to the vast stretch of your eternity. Though the shortness of our lifetime troubles us, the sense of your eternal presence gives us peace. In quiet moments, as we ponder the progressing seasons of our lives, or a dramatic change, or when we are still enough to gaze at the universe revealed to our eyes by night—we may wonder with the psalmist, "Lord, for what do I wait?" We don't know what to make of the unknown that surrounds us when we die. We see little of heaven; it is almost unimaginable. . . . And though the heart begs to know about it, we tell the mind not to attempt to decode your mysteries but to get on with practical living. But, God, you would have us know something of heaven: it is revealed in your Word, the Word of your Son, and in his death and resurrection. We hear that death is a birth to fuller life with you; that pain and sorrow will be banished; that your love will sweep us irresistibly and fully into the light of your presence, and an "eternal weight of glory." Help us to trust the Word revealed to us. For if we do not fear death, we can live our years on earth with greater readiness to follow where your Spirit leads us.

(Psalm 39:4–7)
(2 Corinthians 4:17)

PENTECOST

CALLS TO WORSHIP

1.

LEADER: God's Spirit has been poured upon all flesh.
PEOPLE: That Spirit rests upon us like flames of fire,
LEADER: That we may be light in the world's darkness
PEOPLE: And warmth in the world's coldness.
LEADER: The Spirit has been poured upon us like a mighty wind,
PEOPLE: Refreshing us in love and renewing us in strength,
LEADER: And leading us to serve in love. The Spirit has been poured upon us. Let us worship God in joy!
ALL: Amen.

> Day of Pentecost A,B,C
> Acts 2:1–21

2.

LEADER: The Holy Spirit comes to us as a dove.
PEOPLE: As the dove brought an olive branch to Noah at sea, so you come to us bearing hope and the promise of new beginnings.
LEADER: The Spirit comes as the dove descending upon Jesus.
PEOPLE: So we also bear the Spirit's favor. Rest upon us and uphold us, Spirit of God.
LEADER: The Spirit comes as a dove in flight.
PEOPLE: O Spirit, stir our imagination, and set our hearts to soaring. Lift us up and empower us. Through our worship and work, embrace the world!
ALL: Amen.

> Day of Pentecost A,B,C
> (Genesis 8:10–12)
> (Matthew 3:16–17)

3.

God, whose splendor clothes the world in light, illumines also the shadows of the heart. The Spirit, who refreshes as the wind and warms as flame, dwells within, prompting dream and vision. Christ, whose words set the world to rejoicing, whose touch brought the broken to their feet, still summons to joy and service. Let us sing praise and worship God in love with fresh devotion. Amen.

> Trinity Sunday

4.

Friends, the God whom we love is a demanding God, testing us and pushing us to make and shape our faith, until we, like Abraham, withhold nothing from him. As a teacher pushes students, so God urges us toward growth, completeness, and trust. Let us offer praise to the God who will not let us go!

> Pentecost, Year A
> Genesis 22:1–18

5.

LEADER: This is the house of the Lord, the gate of heaven.
PEOPLE: Surely the Lord is here. We will attend to the voice of God.
LEADER: Christ himself is the door. Let all who would know love enter life through him.
PEOPLE: We draw close to you, O Christ. Open to us the way of salvation. Amen.

> 2nd Pentecost, Year A
> Genesis 28:10–17
> (John 10:1–10)
> (Also 4th Easter, Year A)

6.

LEADER: Our Lord said, "Whoever does the will of God is my brother, and sister, and mother."
PEOPLE: We are members of a common family, sons and daughters cherished by God.
LEADER: Like a kind and generous parent, God provides for our growth. This meal nurtures our souls. We need this meal as much as we need food and drink.
PEOPLE: So we gather around the table to renew our family ties

and to be fed the daily bread, the gift of God.

ALL: Amen.

> 2nd Pentecost, Year B
> Mark 3:35
> (Also World Communion)

7.

LEADER: In the morning when the sun rises
PEOPLE: We shall praise you, O Lord.
LEADER: You have delivered us through every long night
PEOPLE: And given us safe passage across rivers of struggle.
LEADER: The darkness is past; the Light has come.
ALL: In joy we raise our song and prayer to you, O Lord.

> 3rd Pentecost, Year A
> Genesis 32:22–32

8.

Friends, for the eternal God all seasons are autumn, seasons of harvest. So for us, all seasons are times of thanksgiving for God's bountiful provisions, time when we are called to share in the harvest. Let us give praise to God who causes all things to grow, and invites us to share the bounty of divine love. Amen.

> 3rd Pentecost, Year B
> Mark 4:26–34

9.

LEADER: The invitation is extended. Jesus says, "Come to me, all who labor and are heavy laden, and I will give you rest."
PEOPLE: O Jesus, we want to learn from you and work with you, yoked in strength and devotion.
ALL: In this hour give us rest and peace. Then give us to each other and the burdened world. Amen.

> 4th Pentecost, Year A
> Matthew 11:25–30

10.

LEADER: The Living God has brought us this far on our journey.
PEOPLE: God has given bread to the hungry and rest to the weary.
LEADER: God has shown us the future generations—the children in our midst.
PEOPLE: And faithful to the divine promise, God has clothed us with salvation and joy.

LEADER: What more can we ask of our God?
PEOPLE: Bless us and our children forever. Give us the courage
        to pray with trust and serve with joy.
ALL: Amen.

> 7th Pentecost, Year B
> Psalm 132:11–18
> 2 Samuel 7:18–29

11.
The Christ of compassion invites you to rest in the peace of the
Spirit. It is not peace undisturbed by the plight and cries of those
in need, but a peace given in the midst of serving as Christ's
disciples. Come, rest in the peace of the Spirit. Amen.

> 8th Pentecost, Year B
> Mark 6:30–34
> Ephesians 2:11–22

12.
LEADER: Give ear to God's teaching. God will speak in parables
        and utter dark sayings from of old,
PEOPLE: Things that we have heard and known, things our fa-
        thers and mothers have told us. We will not hide them
        from our children: we will tell the coming generation.
LEADER: We will tell the glorious deeds of the Lord, God's
        strength and marvelous works.
ALL: All praise be to God! Amen.

> 10th Pentecost, Year A
> Psalm 78:1–4, adapted

13.
Friends, Christ our Savior has taught us many things, things we
shall spend our lifetimes learning. Perhaps basic among them is
that God is approachable and yearns to befriend us. But we must
indicate our willingness to engage in this best of all friendships.
Therefore, take our Savior's words to heart: ask, seek, knock. You
will be given daily bread, find your heart's desire, and find the door
open. Let us worship our Lord with trust and joy! Amen.

> 11th Pentecost, Year C
> Luke 11:1–13
> Psalm 21:1–7

14.
There are mysteries and marvels and terrors in the universe that
will always elude our understanding. Faced with that which we

cannot comprehend, we should trust God's presence in it all. Though our wisdom may fail, God's care does not. Let us worship God.

(Psalm 131)

15.

All rhythms of time beat in God's great heart:
the time to be born and the time to die,
the time to plant and the time to harvest,
the time to laugh and the time to weep.
All seasons of life are beautiful in their time,
all seasons provide occasions for God's great mercy.
Let us worship God.

(Ecclesiastes 3:1–11)

16.

LEADER: What earthly treasure can we possess that remains unravaged by aging, the elements, or theft?
PEOPLE: There is none. All earthly treasures will fail.
LEADER: But there is an eternal treasure, found through loving and serving Christ.
PEOPLE: In Christ we find the pearl of great price, the unfailing treasure: the richness of God's love.
LEADER: Let us worship God, rejoicing in Christ through whom all things become precious!

13th Pentecost, Year C
Luke 12:32–40

17.

As our Creator spoke to the Hebrews, saying, "I am the Lord your God," so he lays claim to us in a bond of love. As God summoned the people to meet him at the holy mountain, so does he still summon us to gather to worship, to listen to his voice. Let each of you here affirm God's love, declaring in your heart, "Speak, Lord, for your servant hears." Let us worship God together.

14th Pentecost, Year A
Exodus 20:1–20

18.

Friends, have you heard the gentle voice of God murmuring in the undercurrent of ocean, brook, and spring, chortling joy in the song of cardinal and robin, and whispering in the sway of prairie grass and flower? The vaulting trees and streaming sun proclaim the hallowed love of God. Let us worship God who speaks to us in the beauty of all creation!

19.
All creation praises the Creator! In winter the lone crow loudly proclaims God's presence. In spring all the birds unfold a litany of thanksgiving. The insects and frogs of summer continue the chant of blessing. And crickets take up the chorus in fall. In all seasons, God blesses creation. Let us join all God's creatures in singing God's praise!

20.
People of God, we do not live by our own strength alone, but draw life from God. God is our root, deeply planted and firmly established. God anchors all life, and without him there is no life. Let us draw close to God, listening for guidance and trusting in divine love. Let us worship God together.

21.
LEADER: God says, "Listen to me in silence. Let the people renew their strength."
PEOPLE: As we draw near to God, we draw near to each other, helping our neighbors and saying to each other, "Take courage!"
LEADER: You are God's servants, God's friends gathered from the ends of the earth, called from its farthest corners, to whom God says,
PEOPLE: "I have chosen you and not cast you off; fear not, I am with you."
ALL: In thankfulness for God's presence and our strength renewed, we rejoice! Amen.

(Isaiah 41:1, 6, 8–10, adapted)

22.
LEADER: Sing to the Lord a new song. Praise God from the ends of the earth!
PEOPLE: God who created us now says, "Fear not, for I have redeemed you;
LEADER: "I have called you by name, you are mine.
PEOPLE: "When you pass through the waters I will be with you;
LEADER: "And through the rivers, they shall not overwhelm you.
PEOPLE: "For I am the Lord your God, your Savior. You are precious in my eyes."

LEADER: Sing to the Lord a new song and declare God's praise!
ALL: Amen.

(Isaiah 42:10; 43:1–3, adapted)

23.

LEADER: The Mighty One, God the Lord, speaks and summons the earth from the rising of the sun to its setting. God shines forth.
PEOPLE: Hallowed is your name in all the earth, O God.
LEADER: Our God comes; he does not keep silence. Before him is a devouring fire, round him a mighty tempest.
PEOPLE: In word, wind, and fire, come to us, Lord. Renew and refresh us.
LEADER: The Lord calls to the heavens and to the earth; the Lord gathers the faithful and says, "I am your God."
ALL: With thanksgiving for our lives and the gifts of God, we worship in reverence. Amen.

(Psalm 50:1–6)
(Also Transfiguration, Year B)

24.

The Lord who gives peace in all ages has sown seeds of peace to be harvested in ages yet to come. The present is also a field ready for harvest and you are called to share in the labor and its fruits. Let us praise the Lord who calls us to harvest divine peace!

17th Pentecost, Year B
James 3:13–18

25.

The ancient Hebrew stories of our heritage tell us that God talked with Moses face to face, as with a friend. Since the beginning of the world, God has spoken and appeared—sometimes face to face, sometimes in disguise, sometimes subtly, sometimes unmistakably —to confront, comfort, and convert those who will listen to God's word. People of God, we are gathered to praise God in wonder, to open our hearts to divine love and our hands to God's service. Let us praise God with song!

(Exodus 33:11)

26.

LEADER: God has promised: "I will be with you. I will not fail you or forsake you."
PEOPLE: The eternal God is our dwelling place, and underneath

us are the everlasting arms.

ALL: In gratitude for God's love and presence, we worship with joy!

(Deuteronomy 31:6; 33:27)

27.

LEADER: Like God we are not spared the winter of the heart when sorrow weighs heavily upon us.

PEOPLE: Yet we can turn to God, source of life, giver of solace.

LEADER: For having suffered loss, God understands our need

PEOPLE: And sends the Spirit, the Comforter, to bring a fresh source of joy.

ALL: Remembering this, we turn to God, our hope.

22nd Pentecost, Year B
Hebrews 5:1–6

28.

Friends, Christ has crowned our lives with bounty, with gifts immediately recognized and gifts only slowly perceived. Whether we see them or not, Christ continually graces our lives. Therefore draw near to him in joy! Give him praise and thanks! Let us worship God whose gifts shower our lives in splendor!

22nd Pentecost, Year C
Luke 17:11–19
(Psalm 65:11)

29.

Friends, we are called to remember God's gracious acts and sus taining presence. Though we may claim forgetfulness, the heart remembers and no memory is lost. Recall God's graciousness. Call upon God's mercy and claim his love. Let us worship God, who has borne us all along. Amen.

23rd Pentecost, Year B
Deuteronomy 6:1–9

30.

Friends, all generations of God's faithful live in the trust that God wrests abundance out of poverty. Those who withhold nothing from God, giving of their resources and of themselves, find a source of riches that is never spent nor exhausted. Let us worship God who gives to us without ceasing! Amen.

24th Pentecost, Year B
Mark 12:38–44
1 Kings 17:8–16

PRAYERS OF PRAISE

1.

O Spirit of God, you bless our lives with love. Your love is like water poured upon the desert of our hearts; like new wine that warms us with joy; like the wind that drives the chaff away, revealing in us unimagined depth. Your love is like fire, forging holiness in the crucible of our lives. In the blessing of your presence we open our hearts. O God, as water, wind, and fire, flow through us. Amen.

> Day of Pentecost, Year A
> Acts 2:1–21
> John 7:37–39

2.

God of compassion, long is the labor until our second birth. We need a lifetime to grow up into salvation. As a child is slowly formed in the waters of the womb, so are we transfigured by the Spirit, who broods over us, wresting the firmament from the waters of creation. Yours is the travail that propels us into the Light, yours the arms that embrace us from womb to old age. All praise we give you, O God, for you have borne us and carried us. Labor over us still, until we are completely borne into the Light. Amen.

> Trinity Sunday, Year B
> John 3:1–17
> (Isaiah 46:3–4)
> (Also 5th Easter, Year A)
> (1 Peter 2:2)

3.

O God, your Spirit searches the farthest reaches of the universe and the intimate secrets of the human heart. All height and depth, all length and breadth of creation are embraced by your presence. As you know and love us in this depth, help us to understand and love not only what is apparent, but all hidden riches as well. For so shall we discover your presence at the heart of all creation. Amen.

> Pentecost, Year B
> 1 Samuel 16:1–13
> (Also 4th Lent, Year A)

4.

God, whose presence surrounds us, whose home is everywhere, there is no nook to hide where we are out of reach of your love. The gateway to heaven is anywhere we are. In our dreams you whisper promise and hope to our heart. In the waking hours you call to us, "Come, we've work to do." Lord, you speak to us; you are continually with us. Strengthen us to listen to your call and to work with you in all we do. Amen.

2nd Pentecost, Year A
Genesis 28:10–17
(Psalm 139:7–10)

5.

Lord and Giver of Life, as rain erodes the earth, carrying it from fields, through streams, and at last to the oceans, so all of us find our flesh ebbing, worn at last to dust, and our souls returned to the great ocean of your mercy and love. We bear with sorrow the aging that the years bring upon us. But we could greet it with rejoicing, for each day that our creaturely strength and power ebb, our spiritual strength increases. Day after day, you drench us with your eternal Spirit until we are fully transformed into new creatures, reflecting your radiance and love. We praise you, God, for your eternal mercy at work in our lives. Amen.

2nd Pentecost, Year B
2 Corinthians 4:13–5:1

6.

O Compassionate Spirit, when we have been cast into the heart of the desert, with all our resources exhausted, and exiled from hope, you search us out. Rescuing us from our weakness, you call us by name; you restore our strength and give us a vision of future grace that empowers us to live. We praise you, God, for your kindness, as refreshing and blessed as a spring in the midst of the desert. Amen.

(Genesis 21:9–21)

7.

All mysteries of the universe are cached in your great heart, O God, from the silent orbits of the mighty planets to the silent unfolding of grain that feeds the world. From the greatest to the smallest, all wonders, like ill-hid secrets, quietly thunder your glory and joy in all creation. Though we have fathomed many things, our understanding does not diminish your power. Wisdom only reclothes the world in wonder! We praise you, God of earth and all planets, for the irrepressible love that continually washes over us! Amen.

3rd Pentecost, Year B
Mark 4:26–34

8.
Blessed be the Lord, who has watched over us, for we, like Moses among the bulrushes, rely on the vigilance of others and depend on the compassion of others. Blessed be the Lord, who has not given us over to swift currents, but has brought us to a safe haven. O Lord, let us live to praise your name, shepherd your flock, and lead your people to the promised land of your mercy. Amen.

4th Pentecost, Year A
Exodus 1:6–14; 1:22–2:10
Psalm 124

9.
O Living Christ, our lives are voyages of trust through years immense as oceans. Like the sea, our lives are not placid, but rocked by change and storm. Nevertheless, you are with us, and, trusting in you, we can possess a great interior peace. We thank you, God, for your saving presence, and the haven you give to all in distress. Give us joy to praise you through all the hours. Amen.

4th Pentecost, Year B
Mark 4:35–41

10.
Holy God, with deep tenderness you are present in our world, silent but palpable, like the fragrance of a warm summer night; silent but merciful, like ample rains falling upon the fields. In mystery and majesty you have woven your Light and love into the tapestry of our lives. We praise you for love that suffuses our lives, love that like rain permeates and gives life to all it touches. Amen.

11.
God of splendor, like flowers unfolding petal by petal, young birds taking flight, and trees shedding cool shade upon the earth, all the earth ripens in summer toward fullness of being. In the calm and beauty of the morning you call us aside to rest in your care, to trust that the power unfolding in such beauty in the world about us will cause our hearts to blossom in due time as well. Amen.

8th Pentecost, Year B
Mark 6:30–34

12.
Christ, Lord of the Feast, you call us to the table where we are nourished by love. Like the bread and fish never exhausted, your love is never diminished by our need. For abundant provisions, we give you thanks. For your inexpressible gift, we praise you. For love that feeds our souls, we offer you access to our deepest heart. Give us, as you have given yourself, to the world in love. Amen.

> 9th Pentecost, Year B
> John 6:1–15
> (Communion)

13.
God of mercy, we praise you for the hunger you place in our hearts, the longing to find our lives hallowed and gilded by grace; a yearning that impels us to seek, ask, and knock until we find our heart's true desire. O God, you hear our prayers of longing born of the hunger for all that is holy. We praise you for steadfast love, for like a friend at midnight, you will rise to answer us when we call. Amen.

> 11th Pentecost, Year C
> Luke 11:1–13
> Psalm 21:1–7

14.
God, Wondrous Creator, with design and beauty past fathoming, you have lavished grace upon the world. In the shimmering warm light of the sun, and the comforting cool light of the stars, we feel the sheltering closeness of your glory. The stable earth, rustling wind, bright fire, and flowing water bring us close to your elemental, exalted presence. Open to us the gates of Eden once more, for this earth is your garden. Out of its bounty you feed and sustain us, that we may love all creatures born of your breath and Spirit. Amen.

> (Job 36:24; 37:1–14)

15.
Shepherd of all that lives, your loving care is boundless; your mercies sustain all creatures. The whales that play in the ocean sing your praise. The gentle dove is your messenger, and the animals that share our homes are your ministers. With all that is mute and all that has voice, we praise you for the morning and thank you for your care. Amen.

> (Psalm 104:14–30)

16.

Jesus our Savior, born in a borrowed stable and laid to rest in a borrowed tomb, you cherished no dwelling as your own. Such was the poverty that enabled you to give yourself to us, making our hearts your home. You are the cornerstone on whose strength we depend. You are the foundation on whose grace we rest. You are the door bidding us enter the world. We praise you for the refuge we have found in your presence; send us, in your name, to all who are rootless, lost, without rest. Amen.

(John 14:23)

(Also 6th Easter, Year C)

17.

Everlasting God, from age to age and day to day, your love for us never diminishes. Your love knows no special season of abundance nor awaits a favorable mood. You constantly enfold us with extravagant care, and you desire that we simply accept this gift, making your love the center and anchor of our lives. How else shall we live if not grounded in your love? Anchor us, Lord, securely in your presence, and fortify your people with unshakable peace. Amen.

18.

O Lord, like an ageless wave your Spirit flows through us. Your word is the current that carries our lives. At every turn we are blessed and contained by your ancient love that continually and insistently refreshes us. Help us, as we worship, to open our lives to the Light that beams from the dawn of creation, that lights our path, the Light in which all people shall find completion and peace. Amen.

19.

God of mystery and splendor, you find holy joy in giving, bearing the gifts we most need. Into our poverty and emptiness, you bear treasures never to be taken from us, riches nothing can destroy. It is your pleasure to give yourself to us; help us in peace and joy to receive you. Amen.

(Luke 12:29–34)

20.
O Christ, you come to us as the bearer of mercy. And you raise us from troubled depths to the sweet mysteries of wholeness restored. Daily we need this resurrection. Cleanse us in the pools of your grace, and raise us up strengthened, affirmed, to walk with you and declare your power. Amen.

(John 5:2–9)

21.
O God, as a song's familiar rhythm ingrained upon the heart so strangely moves us, or as the supportive words of a friend recur with echoes of affirmation, your Word sounds and resounds within us, bringing comfort and encouragement. The ancient words and story are springs of life to us, overflowing with vitality. O God, with your Word stored within our hearts, there is nothing that we cannot face, no place where we cannot venture; no person that we cannot help but love with the cherishing warmth by which we ourselves are loved. Amen.

22.
Living God, we look at each other and see familiar faces that have ceased to evoke surprise or wonder. We are as predictable as the rising of the sun. And yet, God, because each of us is made in your image, we retain the freshness, energy, and innocence of souls freshly born, and constantly reborn. We are unaccustomed to angels in our midst, unaware of the gifts of others. As the north wind refreshes the sky, so freshen our vision, that in each person we might perceive the shadow of the face of Christ. Amen.

23.
Amid every flood, you, O God, are our helper.
In the ark of your shelter we ride the crest
of every wave that assails us.
Now deepen our trust and by your Spirit
anchor us on the firm foundation
of your boundless love. Amen.

(Genesis 7–8)

24.
O God, though your ways are hidden from our sight, and your messengers often come to us in disguise, there is no question about the reality of your astonishing grace in our lives. We give you thanks for blessings we have recognized and blessings we are slow

to realize. We thank you for mercies plain and mercies concealed. Give us eyes to see your glory, ears to hear your word, and faith to act on holy impulses when no guarantee of results is in sight. Amen.

25.

God of mystery, we cannot presume to know how constantly and in what varied ways you have reached out to befriend us. Sometimes we hear your voice clearly, spelling out guidance. You intercede through the words of a friend. You ask us to answer someone else's prayers. Open us as channels of your healing love. Answer our own prayers for peace and healing. Then open us to the doors of human need, sending us where your work needs to be done. Amen.

26.

O God, in mystery and providence you summon us to lives of pilgrimage, breaking new routes to destinations unforeseen. If we seek to love you, we cannot plan the course of our life in detail, but can only be guided by the mysteries of your direction—signposts that flare like a pillar of fire, lighting our path through the night. For the mysteries of our journey we praise you, O God. Speak your Word of unexpected grace and wisdom to all here gathered. Amen.

27.

O God, you speak in the voice of silence. We praise you not with trumpet but with a subtle song: for rain and shadows, for quiet prairie flowers that no one sees, for squirrels rustling in the leaves. For mysteries of your working too large to fathom, too small to see, we give you praise! Keep us ever attentive to your quiet graces. Amen.

28.

Holy God, most ancient of days, we acknowledge you as the most steadfast presence in our world. All else changes. Flowers blossom, then wither; rivers rise and erode the land; volcanoes slumber, waiting to erupt; the world weathers unrest and violence and yearns for peace; infants are born, and the aged return to the life before and beyond death. All life on this planet ebbs and flows. But you, O Lord, remain constant, showing no variation in your power and love, your meticulous care for each creature. We ask you, Lord, to deliver us from indecision, to make us constant in love and consistent in our care of others and the world. Plant us firmly in the bedrock of your being, that all we do and say may spring forth from your constant strength and diligent love. Amen.

29.

Steadfast Lord, already signs of the changing season greet and haunt us: fading summer flowers; grains and seeds hardening to protect the germ of life against winter's distant freeze; now and then a leaf falling; here and there, leaves flaring crimson. The resurrection that we greeted in spring is fading, drying, and descending back to earth again. You are the Lord of autumn, as much as of summer and spring. In the midst of this diminishing, remind us of forever unfading treasures—your brilliant glory, your love for us, the hope you place within us. Confident that your love weathers all seasons, we lift our hearts in thankful praise! Amen.

30.

Lord of autumn, we hear the measured chirping of crickets, leaves rustling, the gentle ring of rain upon the roof. These quiet sounds accompany our day like music, reminding us that your voice murmurs with a steady undertone of love through all the hours. Keep us attentive to your call that we may praise you with all that is mute and all that has voice. Amen.

15th Pentecost, Year B
Mark 7:31–37

31.

O God, as of old the bright star rises. As of old, the stormy sea is calmed and the immense stone is cast aside. For this is the day that Jesus is born; this the day he rises from death. Now no less than centuries ago Jesus walks among us, heals and prays for us. Now as then, he calls us to love until all are healed. For the blessing of Christ in our midst now, as in Galilee, we give you thanks and praise, O God. Amen.

16th Pentecost, Year C
Hebrews 13:8

32.

Guiding Spirit, your Word comes to us like the song of a bird barely heard. As we listen to identify your voice, we hear only silence. Your Word has always come to people quietly, fleetingly, demanding close attention and much faith. We praise you for those throughout the centuries who have heard what others failed to hear and sensed your intangible presence. Give us faith to trust their witness that we too may know "what no eye has seen nor ear heard, nor the heart conceived, what God has prepared for those who love God." Amen.

(Numbers 22)
(1 Corinthians 2:9)

33.
Giver of all gifts, in billowing clouds that water the earth we know your springs of mercy. In autumn's golden flame we see your radiance and glory. Turn our eyes not only to the splendor all about us, but also to the the gifts you have lavished upon us. Then shall we know that our personal gift stems from the creative Spirit you have placed within us. Amen.

34.
Everlasting God, as gold autumn light blesses the fields, our homes, and all creatures, so does your glory encompass us and your love surround us: a love that neither wanes in the night nor wavers during storms. We praise you for love more wondrous than the turning of color of the trees. Amen.

35.
O God of splendor, in the spring blooming of crocus and tulip, in the summer fanfare of our gardens and fields, in autumn's crimson and gold, and in winter's rest and leanness, we find you at work. You are at work in the seasons of the year, as in the seasons of our lives. After winters of despair, you help us to live again. After summers of fullness and exuberance, you give us the rest and inwardness of winter. In this, a season of harvest and ingathering, help us, O God, to praise you for love that is poured out "in good measure, pressed down, shaken together, running over," a true harvest of bounty. Amen.

(Luke 6:38)

36.
Savior of all the earth's children, you came to us as a little child, to lead us to wisdom and love. And when you grew up you embraced children, telling us that they lead the way into God's kingdom. We praise you for calling us to embody the child's

qualities of tenderness, humility, energy, curiosity, and uncalculated love. As we welcome the children and our lost childlike selves we are even welcoming God, and to this we say Amen!

19th Pentecost, Year B
Mark 10:2–16

37.

We praise you, God, for the hope that flourishes within us. The arid heart hopes for mercy like a flowing stream; those who sow with tears dream of reaping with joy! You turn the evening of tears into morning's joy. Be with us until we come fully into your presence—the place of hope fulfilled, the place of no more thirst nor tears, at home forever in your love. Amen.

22nd Pentecost, Year B
Psalm 126
(Also All Saints, Year A)
(Revelation 7:9–17)
(Also Thanksgiving, Year B)

38.

Wondrous God, our human journey is dwarfed by the immensity of the universe. Your creation is boundless. Yet you care for us, tenderly weeping when one of your creatures is wrested from earth and thrust into heaven. We praise you, merciful God, for compassion as boundless as the universe, yet as intimate as falling tears. We thank you for your love and unity with us in sorrow and in joy. Amen.

All Saints, Year B
John 11:32–44
(Also 5th Lent, Year A)

39.

God of overwhelming mercy, you have claimed each generation of people as your family, fellow workers and heirs of your grace. From the wealth of your storehouses an endless stream of love, mercy, and wisdom has washed over your people. Wave upon wave of endless light sweeps over us. How great are your storehouses, O God, how vast, how varied your gifts! In this hour enable us to open our hearts and receive your gifts. We praise you for the treasure of your love poured out for us and for all, in a thousand ways! Amen.

Thanksgiving

40.

O Christ, you are the king of the ages, reigning in majesty and glory, enthroned in human hearts where you rule in gentleness and love. Until that day when all the earth is filled with your glory and all flesh shall see it together, we pray with hope for the consummation of your kingdom. O Christ, you reign in our hearts with grace and power. Come, reign over the world, that your light may illumine the farthest reaches of the universe as it enlightens our souls. You are the King of Kings. In joy we praise you, Christ our Lord. Amen.

> Last Sunday After Pentecost A,B,C
> Christ the King
> (Isaiah 40:5)

PRAYERS OF CONFESSION OR AFFIRMATION

1.

God, you pour your living Spirit into our lives. We confess that we are not receptive to your presence. You stir us like the unpredictable wind—suggesting astonishing things like feeding and forgiving our enemies, when we feel most uncharitable. You sweep over us like flames of fire, yet we persist in ignoring the light. We remain untouched and unmoved, and so, unloved and unloving. Without your Spirit, we are as lifeless dry bones strewn in the desert. O God, you can bring us to life again—sensitive to the presence and call of your Spirit. Forgive us and make us receptive to your Spirit. Amen.

> Day of Pentecost, Year B
> Ezekiel 37:1–14
> Acts 2:1–21

2.

O God, in wisdom and compassion you discern our innermost thoughts and our holiest desires. You call us to service out of this intimate knowledge and are not swayed by first impressions. We confess that we do not often view others as you view us. We do not see depth, sincerity, and potential, but form snap judgments and refuse to change them. In this way we forfeit friendships and hurt others. Forgive us, God, and teach us to see with the heart and not simply to judge by appearances. Amen.

> Pentecost, Year B
> 1 Samuel 16:1–13

3.

Call to Confession: In our brokenness, we have refused the refuge of God's love. Let us confess the sin that prevents us from accept ing God's love.

God, in your mercy you shelter us as a dove with its wings shelters its young against the storm. If we seek your loving presence, we will always find refuge, refreshment, and the strength to cope with hardship. We confess that we do not always seek your love in times of affliction, for we find despair easier than trust. Forgive us, God. When King Saul was tormented, the soothing melodies of David brought him tranquillity. We confess that we seldom soothe those who are troubled. Instead, we aggravate tensions and fears. We ask your mercy, God, for our failure to offer compassion. Cleanse our hearts of mistrust, and fill us with a love strong enough to offer others refuge. Amen.

> 2nd Pentecost, Year B
> Psalm 57
> 1 Samuel 16:14–23

4.

O God, your love courses through our lives like a flowing river, abundant in grace and power. We confess that we have not stopped to be refreshed by your Spirit. We have bypassed the streams of mercy and in so doing have forfeited the strength you offer your servants. Lord, forgive us. We have dammed up the river of your power with grudges, nursed hurts, and self-pity. We have refused to channel your love to others, especially those we find hard to love. In your mercy, forgive us. Cleanse us of old regrets and ancient wounds; restore us to peace—peace within, peace between friends, and peace in your Spirit. Amen.

> 3rd Pentecost, Year A
> Genesis 32:22–32

5.

Eternal God, day by day your love is borne into the world and into our lives. You work imperceptibly—we cannot see your will working any more than we can watch a seed grow. But you also work steadily, and we have faith that our lives, like the tiny mustard seed, shall at last yield a haven to shelter many. God, you have freely strewn the seeds of blessing into the world. The crop grows despite the obstacles we pose, but it will flourish if we cooperate with you. Grant us renewed trust in your gentle will, which is working for love in the world. Strengthen us to work for the harvest, in the fields that are the people and the events of our lives. Amen.

3rd Pentecost, Year B
Affirmation
Mark 4:26–34

6.

God of Moses and Miriam, we give you thanks for all mysteries of our redemption. Our journey has been blessed by many whom we are unable to remember or to thank. When we were adrift in dangerous situations, some, like Miriam watching over Moses, protected us when we were unable to defend ourselves. Like Miriam, who through courage brought Moses' mother to nurse him, there are those who have taken stands for our welfare. And there are those whose faith, like that of Moses, made such journeys possible. Had they not believed in a promised land and a future of freedom, we could not have endured. We praise you for those who, like Miriam, with song and dance remind us never to take your miraculous acts for granted, but to sing praise to you, giver of all life and salvation. Grant us the faith and strength to accompany others on that arduous journey to the promised land. Amen.

4th Pentecost, Year A
Affirmation
Exodus 1:6–14, 22; 2:1–10
(Micah 6:4)

7.

LEADER: Praise God for love that risks!
PEOPLE: For baby Moses afloat on the Nile and infant Jesus born amid cattle and oxen.
LEADER: God uses fragile beginnings and improbable powerless people to free and to save.
PEOPLE: Pharaoh and Herod and all their kind are confounded; the simple wisdom of God finds its way.
LEADER: God, guard all our perilous beginnings, middles, and endings; rescue us when we are set adrift and harbor us safely.
PEOPLE: Thus shall we marvel in joy at the God who takes chances on our chances!
ALL: Amen.

4th Pentecost, Year A
Affirmation
Exodus 1:6–14, 22· 2:1–10

8.

Amazing God, you have risked so much in entrusting the fulfillment of your promises to such as us. We are reluctant to speak,
like Moses; we are sly like Jacob, backpedaling like Jonah. We
harbor few qualities desirable in saints. Further, we doubt your
methods. A God should work through the strong, powerful, and
wise. Instead, you choose the weak, the simple, the crucified One,
and reluctant servants. You let the whole future of Israel ride
down the river with a crying baby floating in a basket. Your own
Son arrived on earth amid squalor, roamed homeless, and was
despised by town leaders. God, how can you get your work done
this way? You hear our doubts, God. It all boils down to our
feelings of unworthiness and the fear that you might be calling us.
If you would use such fragile vessels as us to bring love, kindness,
and justice into our world, cleanse our hearts, we pray, of fear and
mistrust; and let us know your love that secures the foundation
of our world. Amen.

> 4th Pentecost, Year A
> Exodus 1:6–14, 22; 2:1–10

9.

Call to Confession: As on that evening long ago when Jesus and
the disciples were together in the boat, it is now we who face the
storm and we who doubt Jesus' power. Let us confess our sin.

O Christ, you summoned the disciples to a voyage across a sea at
night. Like them, we hear you inviting us on a voyage of trust. We
cannot see the way; . . . trouble may overtake us. Yet your presence provides haven from the storm. We confess that like the
disciples we are anxious, for you seem asleep to our cries. We
confess that we find the appeal to trust you absurd when we're
frantically bailing to prevent sinking. If you command the wind
and sea, couldn't you give us tranquillity always? Hear us, O Lord.
Rescue us from the fears that threaten to submerge us. Forgive us
and give us your peace. Amen.

> 4th Pentecost, Year B
> Mark 4:35–41

Assurance of Pardon: All who seek forgiveness, trust that the Lord
hears your cries. When we cry to the Lord in our trouble, God
delivers us from our distress, stills the storm and brings us to the
haven of divine mercy. In Jesus Christ, we are forgiven. Amen.

> (Psalm 107:28–30)

10.

Lord of the Sabbath, we confess that we refuse your gift of Sabbath rest. The Sabbath reminds us of your rest after the labor of creation, but we never truly rest from our labors. The Sabbath anticipates eternal rest and joy, but we forfeit the closeness to you that can be ours this day. Forgive us, God. Like the Hebrews seeking manna on the Sabbath but finding none, we find our efforts fruitless until we have rested in the shelter of your grace. Teach us to trust in your providence. Teach us that resting in your Spirit is as necessary as laboring on behalf of the Spirit. And when we forget the promise of Sabbath rest, forgive us and lead us to the still waters where hope and life are restored. Amen.

(Exodus 16:22–30)
(Psalm 23)

Assurance of Pardon: God extends the gracious promise of rest to us: "Come to me, all who are heavy laden, and I will give you rest." Accept the precious gift of Christ's forgiveness and peace. Amen.

(Hebrews 4:1)
(Matthew 11:28)

11.

God of shepherding love, we are born into the world alone. And in solitude we depart from the world at our death. During the precious years in between, we have the gift of countless opportunities to befriend each other. Jesus Christ instructed his disciples to take nothing for the journey, save a shepherd's staff, the symbol of your shepherding care and their responsibility to care for others. In all else he told them to rely on the welcome and kindness of others, and to discount the security that comes from possessions. We thank you, God, for the example of Christ and the disciples, who teach us to value love and our responsibility to others above all else. Grant that we may truly befriend each other, so that no one lives out life in loneliness. Amen.

7th Pentecost, Year B
Affirmation
2 Samuel 7:18–29
Mark 6:7–13

12.

O God, the crow never plows the fields on a tractor, the sparrow never sows or harvests grain. Yet each day they feed at a table spread with abundance and set with love. The iris does not weave cloth; the peony does not sew. Yet they are clothed in splendor and splashed with perfume besides! O God, if you care so much that you feed the birds and clothe the flowers, whose beauty is so fleeting, how much more do you feed our hunger and fit us for life? Teach us to trust in your provision for our daily needs, and deepen our hunger for your sustaining love. Amen.

> Affirmation
> (Matthew 6:25–33)

13.

Lord, Giver of Bread, you have shared the loaves and fishes, bread and wine with all people. You are the gracious host who attends to us all, welcoming and nourishing us. We confess that it is hard to follow your example; it is difficult to be both host and guest. We are grudging hosts who refuse to pour ourselves out for the hungry. We calculate what the merriment will cost us and we await our guests' quick departure. We take for granted our host's preparations and goodwill and fail to express our thanks. O God, forgive our sins against each other. Forgive our sin against you, who meet us at every turn as the compassionate host and the uninvited guest. Amen. ·

> 8th Pentecost, Year A
> Matthew 14:13–21
> (Communion)

14.

Call to Confession: The Bible presents us with flesh-and-blood people who sinned as we sin. In every book we see the shape of our brokenness reflected and we see broken lives made whole. If we confess our sin, we clear the way for God to work within us.

LEADER: O God, scripture is like a mirror in which we see ourselves reflected.

PEOPLE: We are like Mary, who has made a long habit of shirk-
ing duties in favor of wisdom.

LEADER: We whine like Martha, "Tell her to help me!" when the
burden of service saps our strength.

PEOPLE: Like the elder brother we may hold our grudges forever
against a prodigal brother . . .

LEADER: And refuse to recognize God's long-standing mercies in
our own lives.

PEOPLE: Like Martha, we may let our busy lives distract us from the essential and the holy.
LEADER: Help us, God, to sit at Jesus' feet and learn in peace,
PEOPLE: To forget our wounds, to celebrate your work in others,
LEADER: And to serve you with single-mindedness in love.
ALL: Amen.

> 10th Pentecost, Year C
> Luke 10:38–42
> (Luke 15:11–32)

15.

O God, you have revealed yourself to us as a friend worthy of our ultimate trust. You are always available: there is no time when we cannot approach you. You are always generous: there is no gift that we cannot seek from you. As parents would not dream of betraying their child with an evil gift, so there is no hint of malice or betrayal in your dealings with us. As children trust absolutely in their parents' care and provisions, we know you are the source of all joy, all blessing and life; that you want to crown our lives with health and goodness; that you want to give blessings richer than the finest gold. We rejoice in the access we have to you, our dearest friend, through prayer. Make us eager to know you better, and to serve you, by befriending all the world's children. Amen.

> 11th Pentecost, Year C
> Affirmation
> Psalm 21:1–7
> Luke 11:1–13

16.

Merciful Father, we confess we have failed you—spurning the resources of prayer, doubting your power to intervene in human life and world events. We confess we have failed those we love and those who depend upon us—not loving as fully as we can, leaving kind words unsaid, withholding caring actions, doing and saying things that wound others. We confess that we have failed ourselves —making feeble use of our gifts, falling short of our goals, failing to allow ourselves to accept forgiveness for our faults and the grace to begin anew. God, in your unfailing mercy, grant us the peace to part with past failure and the courage graciously to accept the future you offer. Amen.

Assurance of Pardon: God, who is rich in mercy, bids you lift your hearts and realize his presence. See God's immeasurable grace in kindness toward us in Christ! In grace you have been saved through faith. It is the gift of God! Believe and accept the gift: your sins are forgiven. Amen.

(Ephesians 2:4–10, adapted)

17.
So often, God, we doubt your intention and power. We are skeptical that you would want to work through us. We often doubt if you could. We limit you by failing to realize your hidden ways, your access to the depths of our souls, in spite of ourselves. You work through us when we least expect it. What could we accomplish together if we took seriously the call to be your co-workers? Forgive us, Lord, for withholding ourselves from you. Reshape our hearts until every fiber within us yearns to do your will. Amen.

(1 Corinthians 3:9)

18.
Holy God, so often we are like Jonah. We hear your call, then resist your Word, running from you as far as we can. We think that you cannot possibly use us. But we forget that where we see no way, you can create one; that your presence and power can overcome our hesitation and sense of inadequacy; that when you call someone, you also provide gifts for service. Forgive our resistance and excuses. Enable each of us to see where our call lies and to serve you and all your children. Amen.

(Jonah 1–2)

19.
Call to Confession: If we place our trust in human strength alone, we find ourselves in a position of weakness. Let us confess our failure to affirm God's strength in our lives.

(2 Corinthians 12:9–10)

God of all power, you are the source of every gift, all strength and power. We confess that our image of strength is not the Christ, who disappointed all who sought a mighty savior. Rather, our symbol of strength is Samson, who lunged through life by sheer brute force and strong will, with a dauntless courage and superhuman strength that intimidated enemy and friend alike. As we seek to shape our lives in an insecure world, the image of Samson's strength suggests that physical strength can make our lives secure. But there is no ultimate security in sheer strength alone. Teach us, O God, that strength manifest in your Son, our Lord; the gentle strength that comes to fullness in weakness, the power that exists in trusting your Spirit. Amen.

(Judges 16)
(Romans 12:7–10)

Assurance of Pardon: God gives power to the faint and increases the strength of those who have no might. Those who wait for the Lord shall renew their strength. They shall rise up with wings like eagles, they shall run and not be weary, they shall walk and not faint. God knows our weakness and replenishes us to love and serve. In Jesus Christ we are forgiven. Amen.

(Isaiah 40:29, 31, adapted)

20.
Call to Confession: God is more intent on us than we are intent on divine grace. Let us confess our divided hearts.

Loving God, in mystery and grace you sustain us, though we do not often realize your care. We confess that our worries consume our attention, that we put our material needs first, and that we are numb to our spiritual hunger. Jesus has told us that if we seek material things before our spiritual treasure, our priorities are wrong. God, forgive us. Set us free from anxiety, and give us a new trust in your ability to care for us. Amen.

21.
God of unfailing mercy, we acknowledge Christ as the unshakable foundation of our lives. His constant love, his insistent call, and his enduring presence among us quell our anxiety and free us to bear his light into the darkest corners of our world. Yet as much as we believe this, we are reluctant to be used by Christ as stones laid upon the foundation of his life. We do not sacrifice as he did. We reserve ourselves, as if some more important task will soon claim us. And daily we reject your claim upon us as your royal and chosen people. O God, forgive our reluctance to be your servants, and declare again and again your words of mercy until we finally and totally believe. Amen.

(1 Peter 2:2–10)

Assurance of Pardon: God has delivered us from the dominion of darkness and given us to the kingdom of his beloved Son, in whom we have redemption, the forgiveness of sins. Let us give praise to

God, who has qualified us to share in the inheritance of the saints in light.

(Colossians 1:12–14, adapted)

22.

O God, we affirm you as the Word, the God who will not keep quiet. With unmatched eloquence, you summoned into being the earth and all creatures. Then you blessed creation in a voice brimming with love. In the rumble of thunder, in a dreamlike whisper, in angel song; in the voice that shakes the wilderness and the small voice that moves our hearts, we hear you call us to eternal friendship and conversation. Do not let us interrupt that gracious conversation, but keep us attentive to your voice and quick to perceive your call in the events and people that surround us. Amen.

15th Pentecost, Year B
Affirmation
Proverbs 2:1–8
Mark 7:31–37

23.

O God, in love undiminished by generations of people and centuries of time, you care for us as deeply as those who strained to hear Jesus' gracious words and who yearned for his healing touch. Forgive us, for we are slow to trust in your love, unchanged by all history. We have not claimed the ancient story of your love as our own. If we do not see ourselves as the blind, the broken, and the lost, neither can we see ourselves as those whom Jesus found, healed, and claimed as disciples. Have mercy upon us, O God. And make known to us your love in the eternal, unchanging Jesus Christ, our Savior. Amen.

16th Pentecost, Year C
Hebrews 13:1–8

24.

O God, we confess that, like Joseph's brothers, we have been hostile toward those who bear grand dreams. Something about their faith in the vision is exasperating and offensive. We too will strive to conceal the dream or to kill the dreamer. God, have mercy upon us, who cannot bear the wisdom expressed by the servants of the dream. Were we to believe the vision, we would have to take your power seriously and realize that you continuously address our situation. Worse yet, we would have to live the dream—submitting our lives to your wisdom, a wisdom that might well require a lifetime or more to become fully clear. God, forgive us. Dreams bear us into the future—your future—and we are too impatient and untrusting to live out the dream. Give us such trust as Joseph had, in dreams, in your providence, and in life. Amen.

(Genesis 37:1–24)

25.

Lord of peace, like a child at rest, we can dwell peacefully in the world, knowing that you shelter us in your love. As Jesus embraced a child in his arms, so you welcome us as your cherished sons and daughters. Your love gives us the peace that shall sustain us through all life's seasons, from infancy through old age. You endeared yourself to the world as the Christ child. Thus you share the childlike heart and understand the loving, vulnerable child that is our inmost self. Help us to embrace all the earth's children as Christ did, with a ready embrace, willing to work at our love as members of a common family. Amen.

17th Pentecost, Year B
Affirmation
Mark 9:30–37

26.

Call to Confession: God created the heavens, the earth, and all creatures. God who blesses us has also covenanted with the animals. If we dishonor God's creatures, we also dishonor their Creator. Let us confess our sin against God and creation.

Most loving God, Jesus taught that you care for creatures as small as sparrows. And the prophet envisions the fullness of your reign as a peaceable kingdom in which the wolf and the lamb, the calf and the lion shall dwell together. Forgive us the arrogance that assumes that only we, above all God's creatures, possess wisdom and can worship and serve you. Forgive us, God. We remember that you said to subdue the earth and have dominion over every living thing. But we forget that you declared your creatures to be good, that you made a covenant with them, as you did with Noah and his descendants. As Jesus used animals to teach about God's love, enable us to learn from them as well. For we are all creatures, lovingly sustained by the one Creator. Amen.

(Genesis 9:10)
(Job 12:7–12)
(Isaiah 11:6–9)

Assurance of Pardon: God, who values each sparrow, loves us immeasurably more. In Jesus Christ, the Lamb of God, we, God's creatures, are forgiven.

(Matthew 10:29–31)

27.

Loving God, Father of the Prince of Peace, we confess our sorrow at a world where war and rumors of war plague us daily. We confess that we have blocked it trom our minds and live with a false sense of security. For until war is banished and the kingdom of your gentle Shepherd is established, we cannot truly live unafraid. Open our eyes gently, Lord, to the realities of our tense and restless world. Forgive our silence and inaction as reluctant servants of peace. This we pray through Jesus Christ our Lord, who took upon himself our violence, that we might have peace in our hearts and in the world. Amen.

(Mark 13:7)

28.

Call to Confession: The darkness is not dark to God, for the night is as bright as the day. We have not trusted that God's care encompasses all time and space, including the deepest human distress. Let us confess our sin.

(Psalm 139:7–12)

Giver of darkness and light, yours are the height and depth, the fullness and emptiness, the sorrow and joy of existence. We limit you, God, by presuming that you are present only where there is light. We confess that we are as blind as Balaam to the dark side of your presence. We resist believing that your Word can be "no" as well as "yes," that you close doors as well as open them. We see that you bring light to bless, but fail to see that you can also bring darkness to teach us, as you did to Saul. We plunge through obstacles, unwilling as Balaam to admit that our problem might be a gift in disguise. God, help us to consider your purpose in that which bewilders us. Forgive us and heal us of the mistrust which has forgotten that we are held in your hands. Amen.

(Numbers 22)

Assurance of Pardon: Nowhere in creation can we escape the boundaries of God's loving care. God is present in our greatest joy and undergirds us in our deepest sorrow. Accept the forgiveness of God through Christ our Savior. Face the darkness and light of your day with the trust that God holds you close, never to let you go. Amen.

(Psalm 139:7–12)
(Also 5th Epiphany, Year C)

29.

Call to Confession: Families gather around the dinner table to share a meal, to share their lives. This morning as the global family of Christians gather to share the meal of our Lord, we are painfully aware that many are missing. And many who are at the Lord's Table squabble with each other. Let us confess to God the brokenness of the Christian family, and in silent prayer, pray for God's peace.

Loving Creator, you are God of all the families of the earth. And Christ declared all the faithful to be his brothers and sisters. We are a family that spans the world, but we confess that too often we embody the worst aspects of families. We declare whole nations to be black sheep, cast out of the circle of family concern. The struggles and rivalry of Jacob and Esau pale before our daily quarrels which have shattered global peace. And like family members who lose track of one another, we fail to nurture the bonds of affection. God, have mercy upon the members of this broken family that spans all oceans and lands. And forgive us when we treat any one of them as other than a sister or brother in Christ. Amen.

World Communion
(Mark 3:35)
(Jeremiah 31:1)

30.

LEADER: Generous God, you crown our lives with your bounty,
PEOPLE: And we take your gifts as our due, without appreciation.
LEADER: We are like the ten lepers cleansed by Jesus: Ten are healed, only one gives thanks.
PEOPLE: Ten have been blessed, only one turns in joy to bless the giver.
LEADER: We are the nine: three do not recognize that they have been healed; three have seen the gift and are scared of grace; three recognize the change and credit a change of luck.
PEOPLE: We are the nine, blind to God's gifts. We are the nine,

silent before a gift too great to fathom.
LEADER: Christ, have mercy upon us.
PEOPLE: Lord, have mercy upon us.
ALL: Amen.

(Psalm 65:11)

Assurance of Pardon: Christ neither keeps score of our failures nor counts grudges against us. As he waited for one leper to return to him in joy, so does he stand ready to receive us. Return to Christ in gratitude, for in him your sins are forgiven. Amen.

22nd Pentecost, Year C
Luke 17:11–19

31.

Call to Confession: Life brings seasons of weeping and joy, but we often live in sorrow's everlasting winter, unwilling to greet the springtime of laughter and wonder, unable to joyfully praise God for life. Let us confess our winter hearts.

God, our Savior's life was a journey of tears and joy. He knew the numbing agony of grief and the small frustrations that beset us. He plumbed the depths of sorrow and the abyss of death. But he also beheld the joyful smile of those with sight restored, felt the joy of feeding the hungry in spirit, and on resurrection morning, rose to everlasting joy. We confess that we have failed to live in the hope that our Redeemer sets before us. We view frustration and suffering as permanent features of our lives. We have ceased to expect great things from you; we no longer wait patiently for the dawn of promise when joy will fill our hearts to overflowing. O God, forgive our lack of trust. Restore us to the hope that knows the day shall come when we may greet our neighbors and you with shouts of joy! Amen.

22nd Pentecost, Year B
Psalm 126

32.

God, we affirm you as the God whose love and mercy are unfailing. When we have spent all our strength or resources, we find that if we turn to you, you take the little we have and transform it into abundance. When we confess our poverty, you reveal that we are rich, inheritors of a vast treasure of love. As a poor widow was willing to spend all that she had, increase in us the love which does not count the cost, but spends it freely. Remind us that in Christ Jesus you give us a treasure beyond price! Amen.

> 24th Pentecost, Year B
> Affirmation
> 1 Kings 17:8–16
> Mark 12:38–44

33.

LEADER: O God, all over the world Jesus finds the lost and dines with sinners.

PEOPLE: All over the world are those like Zacchaeus, who want merely to glimpse Jesus, but find their lives transformed.

LEADER: The burden is on us now: we are among those who murmured against Zacchaeus, resenting Jesus' invitation to his kind.

PEOPLE: We confess that we think tomorrow Zacchaeus will be back to his old tricks, forgetting promises.

LEADER: But in Jesus' eyes, Zacchaeus has regained full stature.

PEOPLE: Lord, forgive us. We fail to recognize that your love can change lives.

LEADER: Enable us to respond to your surprising blessing, not our low expectations.

ALL: Amen.

> 25th Pentecost, Year C
> Luke 19:1–10

Assurance of Pardon: We can trust God's promise of mercy which is affirmed in Christ. Jesus said, "Your sins are forgiven." This is indeed good news. Amen.

PASTORAL PRAYERS

1.

O God, your Spirit is intertwined with ours in ways we can scarcely fathom: You are the vine, we the branches. As we remain immersed in your inexhaustible love and depth we are given strength and joy in life. We praise you, God, that you have given all people the precious gift of your Spirit. We pray that we might experience the Spirit's presence more fully, for we see but dimly, hear but faintly, and scarcely feel the brush of your sheltering wings. To those who remain suspicious of joy, come, O Spirit, with love like wine. To those whose lives remain untouched by hope, come, O Spirit, bearing the mysterious suggestions of dream and vision. To those caught in the small circle of self-concern, come as fire and kindle compassion as intense as that of Jesus. To those who feel unworthy of being your servants, O Spirit, come as gracefully as the cooling breeze and claim your servants.

> Day of Pentecost A,B,C
> Acts 2:1–21

2.

O God, we have gathered close to you, seeking refuge in the strength and wisdom of your sheltering presence. We have never known your love to wane or to fail us. Whether we are strong in faith and diligent in service, or if we are disheartened, burdened, seeking solace and compassion from others—strong and weak alike, we find that your eternal love feeds our great hunger and replenishes us with love and endurance. We think of those we know who, like Saul, suffer some private anguish, and we pray that you would give them your peace and renew their hope. We ask you to strengthen us, giving us courage to refresh their weary lives by some personal gesture. Use the gift you have given us, O God, to relieve their burdens and refresh their spirits.

> 2nd Pentecost, Year B
> Psalm 57
> 1 Samuel 16:14–23

3.

Loving God, you are not far from any one of us, but we distance ourselves from you by neglect of prayer, busy schedules, worrying minds, and a short horizon of hope. How often we have closed the door on you without even intending to, leaving conversation with you out of our daily lives. If we have not done so before, help us now to make room and time for prayer. Give to us the sense that time spent in prayer is not duty but our daily bread, and that the fruits of silence before you are far richer than anything we might otherwise do with our time.

4.

O God, your Spirit works without ceasing, flowing as a great river through our lives. We have felt the power of your Spirit seeking us out, dredging us up from despair and lifting us on currents of grace and light. We find that we cannot stay still but are borne by your Spirit to encounters long avoided and to insights long resisted. We praise you, O God, for grace abundant as a mighty river. Have mercy upon us who have endured long, dark nights in struggle, when the masks of self-deception are slowly lifted from our hearts under the searing light of truth and self-judgment. Help us to remember, God, that you never abandon us to our deception, but work in us through the dark nights. You bring us at last to dawn, where, graced by the light of your face, we find ourselves embraced and healed. O God, keep us ever close to your great river of grace and blessing.

3rd Pentecost, Year A
Genesis 32:22–32

5.

O God, the struggles between dawn and dusk are hard, but perhaps the most fierce struggles occur between dusk and dawn. As Jacob crossed the river and met his adversary in solitude, we also cross over into a shadowy realm of struggle during the nocturnal hours. Give us wisdom, God, to discern our enemy's nature. Are we fighting angels? Resisting love? Or are we battling our coward self at last, routing the side of ourself that has always taken detours, run from encounters, and resisted growth? When at last day breaks, give us your blessing. Gently turn us to face our world and our destiny with humility, with a greater capacity for forgiveness and for love.

3rd Pentecost, Year A
Genesis 32:22–32

6.

Christ of all the ages, we look to you to save us. When the storm winds rise, we seek the shelter of your peaceful presence. When the waters threaten to swamp us, we seek the solid anchor of your love. O Christ, do not sleep through our troubles, but awake and save us! Even as we call you to attention, we admit that we are like unconscious dreamers, drifting through our lives unaware that you share our lives with an intimacy that would astound us if we were to become aware of you. We are in the same boat, and you will not abandon us to the storm. Awaken us, O Christ, to the fact that we dwell in the shelter of your presence. Even as you crossed the sea through the night to rescue one man from his torment, we should venture to help those near or distant, despite any danger or sacrifice. Awaken us to hear the call of those who cry, and give us the strength to undertake voyages of trust to those

who need us. Christ of all the ages, strengthen our trust in you,
in each other, and in ourselves.

4th Pentecost, Year B
Mark 4:35–41 (5:1–13)

7.

O God, each of us is haunted by questions we have addressed to
you. Like Elijah we meet with silence. Sometimes it is a silence in
which we discern your answer; sometimes the silence is an absence
that yields no reassurance. We ask that in your time you would
make plain the answers to our questions. We ask the faith and
patience to wait until you reveal them to us. God, we bring before
you all those who test you by demanding signs and miracles, yet
have not the eyes of faith to perceive your grace, so richly embedded in our lives. We bring before you those who have ceased to
ask questions. We pray that your Spirit would move them again
to that interior dialogue with you that is the mark of your disciples
throughout all generations.

6th Pentecost, Year C
1 Kings 19:9–14

8.

O Holy One, in ancient days you revealed your presence and
power by grand intervention, sweeping back the seas that your
chosen people might safely pass beyond their pursuers, or delug-
ing the earth with the flood. Your people perceived your power
on an awesome scale. Your ways were visible. You appeared to
Moses in a flaming bush and woke the prophets through dreams
and messengers. We have grown accustomed to these stories of
miracle and spectacle. Even Jesus walked on water, fed five thousand from a small basket of food, brought the dead to life, and
finally burst the bonds of death itself. God, is it any wonder that
you seem silent and hidden to us? Our life is unmarked by grand,
cosmic signs of your presence. We are hungry for some direct
revelation—a radiant light, a flickering glimpse of your face, the
world hung by its heels for an instant. We hunger to know you,
God. Why can't we see your influence in our lives? We remember
the voices of prophets past, your marvelous acts in history, and
the miracle of Christ. But we have forgotten part of the story: You
are not in the earthquake, wind, and fire; not always extravagant
and showy after all. You come on silent wings as a still small voice,
a whisper of truth, an intuition of someone's need, a quiet courageous impulse, a silent nudge, and in dream or vision. In our thirst
for miracle, we overlook the most daily of miracles, and we neglect

the opportunity to seek your hidden face in moments of prayer. O God, give us a thirst and an openness to meet you in your subtle and quiet ways.

6th Pentecost, Year C
1 Kings 19:9–14
(Isaiah 64:1–4)

9.

O God, like a mighty river, your word and presence flow through our lives. Your waters give us life, refresh us, and carry us on our journey through the winding years. We thank you for Jesus Christ, in whom we perceive your love brimming over for all humanity. We thank you that during the troubled times of our lives, you have been a bridge across turbulent waters. We could not have forded them on our own strength, but only through your mercy. We thank you for helping us to endure, and we ask your saving presence for all who face calamity. Like raging floodwaters before whose power we are helpless, the enemies of peace and love have overrun our world. Alone, we cannot overcome their force. Only you, O God, can stem the floods of violence that threaten to overrun the nations. Stir up your power, O God, and come to save us!

10.

Merciful God, your strongest saints have been people who in tragedy and misfortune were able to summon up their innate strength, and who found their faith renewed. Hagar was such a saint—suffering abuse and exile, watching her child face death. Yet you provided for her an oasis and were for her a source of strength and compassion. As you ministered to Hagar and Ishmael in the wilderness, nourish us also as we face weakness and despair.

The strongest saints had their times of weakness when they were hardly examples to follow. Sarah lacked the patience to wait until you fulfilled your promise to give her a child. She took matters into her own hands, using her servant Hagar as a tool for her own ends, then abused her when the task was complete. Have mercy, Lord, on all your headstrong saints, all who see others as instruments for gain, and all who abuse those closest to them. Nor was Abraham a model of faith. He passively stood by as Sarah hatched her plot to subvert your will. In apathy and powerlessness, he condoned Sarah's harsh treatment of Hagar. Later he dispatched Hagar into desert exile, playing an active role in her misfortune.

Have mercy upon us all when we passively approve jealous acts and violence, and when we hurt each other.

O God, we share the weaknesses of Abraham and Sarah—passivity, mistrust, cruelty. But we also share the strength that made them heirs of your promise: a lasting trust in your ultimate faithfulness. Forgive us our faults and give us trust and strength always to treat others as heirs of your promised goodness.

(Genesis 16:1–6; 21:9–21)

11.

Christ our Savior, you are the Lord of the waters, the waters of baptism and rebirth. By your words hope crests within our hearts, and by the waves of your mercy we are remade, until reality fits our most cherished dreams. We thank you that you come to us, making us new, rekindling hope. Lord of the waters, we pray for all caught in deep pools of despair, mired by passivity and long habit. As you rescued your own disciples from troubled ocean currents, so save our brothers and sisters from the dangerous depths within. In your presence, hopelessness does not ensnare. O Jesus, draw near to all who are of faint hope. Lord of the waters, just as you bring rebirth to individuals, we pray for your healing within nations. Drowning in red seas of violence, retribution, hunger, drought, and sickness, we pray that you would seize the leaders of lands across the oceans with words of wisdom, words of healing, words they cannot ignore. Until the day when peace inhabits every heart and the waters cease to be rivers of tears, we lift this our prayer: Christ our Lord, bring peace to earth.

(John 5:2–9)

12.

Here we are, God, deep in our summer's content.
Lulled and laid low by the heat and sweet breeze,
we neither stir nor seek.
We have hung up the burden of prayers
like laundry fluttering in the wind,
till desire is dry.
This is our season of stasis, this the reign of sameness.
How then shall we ask, knock, seek?
We cannot dream of being fervent,
much less bend our wills
to the efforts of prayer and holy expectation.
God, have mercy upon us.

Will you wait until the lethargy has lifted?
Would you bound to your feet,
if we were to cry this moment, "Come, Lord"?
Would you listen in the still depths of night
when the world is sleeping,
if we were to awake to our plight and need?
Steadfast and wakeful Lord, companion of all hours,
you are attentive to us, never slumbering.
Stir us from our summer's content and listlessness
until our heart's desire is the fervent search for your peace,
not only for ourselves
but for all hearts in all places.

> 11th Pentecost, Year C
> Psalm 21:1–7
> Luke 11:1–13

13.

We live in a strange world, God, where strangers bear little responsibility for each other. We do not correct each other's children; we do not personally reprimand those who violate law. The ties that once bound all people have been broken. The time is past when hospitality was the rule and we cared for sojourners and strangers as much as our own kin. We are left with a yearning for closeness and caring, to be our brother's and sister's keeper, and to be shepherded in return. O God, we are lonely. Will you help us to make connections with others? Press upon us the great need to be lovingly responsible to all we meet. Come to us in our loneliness, bind up our wounds, and give us the strength of your presence.

> (Genesis 4:1–16)

14.

O God, bear with us, please.
We are slothful and catty.
We have little patience with things that dog us
and egg us on.
We hog the earth's resources, then play possum
when we are called to account for our piggishness.
We are cowed by powers that would just as soon we clam up,
failing to go to bat for those who are floundering.
Life is such a zoo sometimes!
O God, bear with us.
Make us wise as serpents, innocent as doves.

Like the dove, may we be signs of your presence
to a badgered world.
May we rest as easily in your care as a lamb
under the eyes of the shepherd.
Dear God, bear with us and all creatures.
Draw us close to everything that stammers
and croaks your praise. Amen.

15.

Lord of the harvest, as farmers patiently wait over the barren soil,
so you have sown in hope to reap a harvest of love. We thank you,
God, for your faith in us and your labor to increase our faithfulness. O Lord, even as the seed that must fall to earth in order to
yield new life, you were buried and now are risen. We find that
unfailing hope in you resurrects us each day. Branches severed
from the root die and bear no fruit. Only connected to each other
and united through Christ do we yield a rich harvest. We thank
you, Lord, that as branches bound to the root, we need each other
and you to flourish. Give us that sense of gratitude in which each
person is cherished as indispensable to the life and happiness of
all others. Lord of the harvest, in dazzling variety you have blessed
us. Hear us as we thank you for your abundance. In gratitude let
us count and savor our blessings . . . *(silent prayer)*. God, it is by
your hand that we exist and through your mercy that we live. For
your bounty which crowns our lives, we thank you with joy!

> (John 12:24)
> (John 15:1–11)
> (Psalm 65:11)
> (Also 5th Easter, Year B)

16.

O God, in times of prayer and introspection we look deeply inside
ourselves. We find memories both haunting and sweet, memories
we choose to forget, but cannot. These memories are immune to
surgery, are never lost, and are always with us. God, we believe
that you work in ways unfathomable to our minds; that you can
work to heal us. As you use your power to affirm and strengthen
us, use your power to heal memories that haunt, weaken, and hurt
us. Speak to us of your love. Through the ingrained images and
stories of your ancient Word, heal and comfort us. Like diamonds
embedded in the rock of the earth, let your Word shine within us,
riches in the midst of rubble. Trusting in your faithfulness to your
promise of love, we thank you that you have already begun the
work for which we pray.

17.
God, in you alone is fullness of being. All else is hollow and empty. Sometimes we feel this emptiness and a vague yearning for what we cannot name. We look around for what is missing. And if we look deep enough we discover that it is you, whose absence in our life is so painful. We have neglected to invite you in. You stand outside, gently knocking, trying to gain our attention and enter our hearts. How could we have neglected to welcome such a visitor? Wait no more, God. Come, dwell in our hearts, that our joy may be complete.

(Revelation 3:20)

18.
Merciful God, though we listen attentively for your voice in prayer and scripture, we sometimes hear only half of what you have to tell us, unable or unwilling to hear the rest. We readily hear that we are sinners, that our life is a journey from dust to dust; but we fail to hear your affirmations: that we are made in your image, crowned with glory; that each day we are transfigured a little more into the likeness of Christ; that we are your fellow workers and a temple of your Spirit. O God, how can we have failed to hear that you are for us, sustaining us with a love that will never cease? O God, make us confident of your love, poured into us, and make us eager to use the gifts you have given.

19.
O Christ, there are many deserts in our lives, many long dark nights, many stark silences, when we neither hear your voice nor feel your presence. In these times we need to know that you are with us. Teach us patience, Lord. In the winter of our spirit, teach us trust. As the earth in winter does not die, but prepares for the return of spring and growth, so you do not leave us alone, but work within us as much when we're unaware as when we're aware of your presence. You loved us first, O Lord, long before we heard your voice. We can lean on your love and there find strength. O Christ, draw us into the light of your mercy. Heal us of doubt and fear, plant the seed of hope, and harvest in us the rich fruit of your love.

(1 John 4:19)

20.

Lord Jesus, you have told us that we may freely approach God, letting our needs be known. You tell us not to be shy in asking, but to be forthright about our desires. How can we be so frank and assuming with God? We even hesitate to ask for what we need from those we love. But, Jesus, you have given us your word that God stands waiting to help. You bid us make our requests known, promising that joy and gifts await our asking. Grant us, God, the persistence in prayer to cooperate with you in our request, the patience with which to await your timing, the discernment to know whether the thing we seek is for good or for harm. In joyful hope and gratitude we pray.

(Matthew 7:1–11)

21.

Holy God, we stare into the face of silent Mystery enveloping our lives. Our questions, dropped like coins into a well, disappear into a realm which we cannot fathom or see. Have you heard our questions, cried out at midnight? The ravaging doubts that haunt our daylight hours? The pain we bear for those we love who are trapped in confusion, burdened by pain and sickness? We have spent ourselves, pouring out complaints to you, O God, begging your mercy, begging your direction, intervention. We have prayed until we have no hope left, nor words with which to address you. In the end, all of us are left silent, staring into the Mystery, which, like the silent starry sky, showers our lives with radiant darkness.

O God, bid us rest in your love. Bid us listen to the deepest heart of ourselves where you wait in readiness. Then, feed us with the peace of your presence, the bread of your love; bid us be refreshed. Stopping to listen, we will hear your answer. Lingering in your presence, we will receive your love. We thank you, God, for the hope we have of grace given in time of hardship.

22.

God, at every turn you speak to us. Not so much in visions in quiet places, as in encounters with hidden angels. But it is easy to attribute our sudden impulse to some act of compassion to our own goodness of heart. But who does not know that God is our prompter in the wings, who, like a good prompter, remains unnoticed? God works through us for love, even when we are unwitting vehicles of grace. Make us conscious, God, of your presence and voice, so that we can do more.

23.

Christ of Bethlehem, Nazareth, Galilee, and Gethsemane, your entire life shines before us like a cathedral window—each story of your life etched in vivid eternal color, transparent to the love of God. In your birth, boyhood, and ministry, in your suffering and resurrection, we see signs of God's favor and blessing for all generations. Indeed, your every word and gesture speaks to us of a God whose love sustains us at every turn. We need no piercing trumpet call, no thunder, no angel chorus to call our attention to the presence of God. For you have shown us more than enough to trust. In your compassionate life, your suffering with us in hardship, in unexpected grace given in our perplexity, we have signs enough of your favor and presence. O Christ of Bethlehem, be born within us. Christ of Nazareth, mature us in every grace. Christ of Galilee, help us to labor with you. Christ of Gethsemane, be with us in sorrow and hardship. Raise us with you, through small deaths and death itself, to the splendor of God's exalted love, manifest in every creature in every place.

(Exodus 20:18–20)
(John 4:46–50)

24.

Dearest God, like our parents who loved us before we were born, you have cradled us in your great heart; loving us, providing for us, before we ever had memories of your care. We thank you for loving us when we were helpless, vulnerable, capable of giving little that the world holds in high esteem.

Since we were once children, it should not be so hard to remember what childhood is like. We remember childhood as a time of indignities, small daily humiliations, clumsiness, and the realization of how little we knew when compared with the wise adults all around us. But just because we are grown and wise is no reason to forget the terrors of being small and needy. Jesus said we must see in each person the child who is hungry for kindness and affection. Then, following Jesus, we must embrace them all with encompassing love.

Help us, God, in welcoming children and all like them, to find you in the eyes of all whom we meet.

17th Pentecost, Year B
Mark 9:30–37

25

God of all the families of the world, for most of us it is enough
to love but a few people deeply: spouse, child, parents. But your
love is not an exclusive love. As loving parents know when it is
time to let go of their children, giving them as gifts to the world,
you let go of Christ, so that all people in all times and places could
come to know your great parental love. You have given Jesus
Christ to us as Savior, as friend, as brother. And in Christ we have
indeed found ourselves at home in a family whose generations
reach back to the ancient ones of our faith, and forward to generations yet to come. We thank you, God, for your sublime love that
reaches out powerfully to uphold the universe, yet intimately
sustains each one of us. We thank you for Jesus Christ, who greets
each person as brother or sister, and summons us to recognize
each other as family.

> 19th Pentecost, Year B
> Mark 10:2–16
> (World Communion)
> (Jeremiah 31:1)

26.

O God, another morning has dawned, another night has fled. With
the rising sun, all our dreams, like mist upon the fields, evaporate
and are remembered no more. Our elusive dreams suggest the
manner of your presence—capturing our hearts with the promise
of a love and richness just beyond our reach and our sight. Help
us to live out the dreams you have placed within our hearts. Help
us to live as servants of the dream, trusting in your will and power,
however faint the signs of them may be.

In all ages there are those, like Joseph's brothers, who despise the
dreamer and reject the message of the dream. Preserve us from
their disbelief and mistrust. Deliver us from the jealousy of others'
guiding dreams that would prevent us from perceiving your gracious word in our own hearts.

O Lord, we are drawn to you as a flower bends to meet the sun.
We are drawn to you, source of our life. Preserve us from any
feeling or act which would sever our vital connection with you
Strengthen us to love you and each other always.

> (Genesis 37:1–24)

27.

Loving God, we are not fond of the hard side of your love that stops us, closes doors, and gives no reason for events that cause pain. Who among us is willing to admit that "God said no" when our hope is for movement, progress, and joy? Which of us is patient enough to endure the shadows that surround us? Brave enough to endure the trials thrust upon us? And faithful enough to trust you through it all? Perhaps none of us alone possesses that strength and trust. We look to you, O God, giver of both darkness and light, to sustain us through that which we cannot endure alone.

We cannot be fond of the deep shadows of your vast heart, mysterious God. But we can trust that you, in your wisdom, will someday reveal how all things have worked for good. We cannot favor obstacles to our fondest dreams, but we can patiently abide them. We can help others facing your mysterious "no" to endure somehow, and perhaps along the way discover together the wisdom of your secret intent. We must abhor the abysses of darkness visible in those who are flagrantly wicked and bring destruction and suffering. And in outrage, we cry out to you for justice for the world.

Mysterious, loving God, hear our prayer. Help us learn to trust at all times, however dim the light may seem.

> (Romans 8:28)
> (Numbers 22)

28.

Sometimes, God, our lives are so restless and busy that we take little time to reach out to you. It is then that you have little choice but to reach out to us in the only quiet place that remains in our lives—while we lie peacefully asleep. Then in our dim dreams you find entrance to our heart, teaching and feeding us all that you wanted to give us while we ran about during the day, unwilling to stop and simply receive your gifts.

While we are thankful for those occasional dreams that wake us up to your presence, we're ashamed that you can reach us only while we're unconscious. We want to meet you in the waking hours, but find it hard to be quiet and still. Help us, God, during this coming week, to take time to pray, to speak with and listen to you, our dearest friend.

> 21st Pentecost, Year A
> Psalm 127:2

29.

O God, this is the hard autumn season. The muted sun, colorless
trees, and cold wind drift over us like low wet clouds. The gentle
beauty and balm of spring is forgotten; the exuberance of summer
is over. We are descending into the barren winter months. As we
see the stark outlines of trees and feel the cold, it is easy to see the
season reflected in ourselves: our small defeats irritate us, and we
stumble headlong over large failures we thought we had buried.
It is easy to despair, easy to give up hope, easy to feel that your
will has a sinister quality to it. O God, this is the season in which
we have a fierce need for the warmth and light of your presence
—a time in which we need your assurance, a time in which we
need you to prod us to loving care of our neighbor lest we fall into
hibernation. God, you have promised that you will neither fail nor
forsake us, that your Spirit is always near. Come to us in the
mysterious grace which we cannot command, but can only receive.

(Deuteronomy 31:6)
(Hebrews 13:5)

30.

Most merciful God, until the day when war ceases to rage between
the nations of the earth, until the day when disease and starvation
no longer prey upon your people, until that day when we are
healed of our divisions, we wait and pray in hope for the graceful
rule of Christ our King. O God, your kingdom come!

Christ, King of the ages, you seek to be king of our hearts as well.
Move us to love you and to serve you in all that we do and all that
we are. So rule in love and grace within us that, convinced of your
power, others will come to acknowledge you as the Lord and giver
of life.

Christ our Lord, we pray to you. In silence we come before you,
awaiting your presence and your word. Come to those places and
people we name before you in silent prayer. . . .

Last Sunday After Pentecost A,B,C
Christ the King

31.

O Jesus, you found peace and a restoration of your energy in the
gently sloping hills of Galilee. The gentle waves of the lake were
so soothing they could lull you to sleep. You gazed at the meadow

flowers and the fields of grain and found common plants to be signs of God's wondrous and extravagant care for all creation. You call us to consider the lilies: to rest in the trust that God who clothes the flowers that bloom but a day will surely look after us as well. O Jesus, just as you spoke these gracious words on the hills about Galilee, you still offer the invitation to rest in the peace of God's care. Release us from the fears that constrain us and deny us delight in God's festive spirit. Help us to live with joy in the blessing of each day. As we find ourselves renewed by your living Spirit, send us to help the careworn find the peace of your presence. Amen.

Thanksgiving, Year B
Matthew 6:25–33

ALL SEASONS

UNISON PRAYERS

Advent

1.

O God, for aged Moses the decades of wilderness journey led just to the brink of promise. But we do not look from the desolate mountain into a land of promise we cannot enter. The season of longing has ended; the season of promise fulfilled has come. In the love given us through Christ all our journeys lead home; all the longing of our solitude is fulfilled. Thank you, God, for promise fulfilled in our lifetime. Amen.

> 1st Advent, Year C
> (Deuteronomy 34:1–6)
> (Jeremiah 33:14–16)
> Luke 21:25–36

2.

All the earth is a cradle of Presence, every heart an infant needing shelter. O God, who in tender delight assumed our hungering flesh in the child Jesus, succor all the earth's children, and open wide our hearts and arms that we may embrace them all as your holy and cherished children. Amen.

Epiphany

3.

O Christ, when joy has run dry like wine whose supply is consumed, come to us. Fill our emptiness and transform our staleness, that we may brim with your delectable love. This we pray in the confidence that you are the Vine, ever-fruitful source of life and joy. Amen.

> 2nd Epiphany, Year C
> John 2:1–11

Lent

4.
God, help us to see the rainbow sign,
the arch of your promise
over our lives.
Help us to trust that amid all floods
You will guide us
to the shores of your kingdom. Amen.

> 1st Lent, Year B
> Genesis 9:8–17

5.
We understand, God, that loving you does not grant us an exemption from harm or crisis. As your Spirit drove Jesus into the desert, you may propel us into harsh territory. May we emerge from our trials strengthened by greater awareness of your mercy and the preciousness of life, and blessed with the compassion to comfort all who suffer affliction. Amen.

> 1st Lent, Year B
> Mark 1:9–15

6.
Creator of the sun and moon and stars, you have always set the stars before us, bright with promise in the night sky. You led Abraham under the starry sky to reassure him; the Magi found Jesus by the light of a wandering star. As we lift our eyes to the stars, our thoughts are lifted to your infinite power and the wonder of your care. When we are mired in doubt, bid us number the stars and know that you who set the constellations can also give hope to our hearts. Amen.

> 2nd Lent, Year C
> Genesis 15:1–12

7.
O God, in all ages you have offered surprising and gracious provision for your people. Even though we grumble and doubt like the people of Israel, your love bounteously sustains us, like water from the rock, quenching our thirst and meeting our need. We thank

you that in Jesus Christ you come to refresh and renew us, as cool water refreshes those who are weary. Jesus offers us divine love as continuous as a spring, flowing with mercy. Help us, like the woman at the well, to accept his gift and joyfully tell others that he is our fountain of joy. Amen.

> 3rd Lent, Year A
> Exodus 17:3–7
> John 4:5–26

8.
O God, no more than Jesus are we permitted to settle in. He was not at home in the world; exile was the pattern of his life. His family found no room at the inn. They were forced to flee their country for their lives. Jesus counted no place as home and had nowhere to lay his head. All his life he wandered. As a final mark of his exile, he was crucified by the people he had loved. No more than Jesus are we permitted to settle in. As disciples, our only home is the shelter of Jesus' love and the love we give each other. Teach us, O God, that all else is cross and exile. Teach us compassion for those in exile, for those whose lives are a harsh and unfamiliar country. Amen.

> 4th Lent, Year B
> 2 Chronicles 36:14–21
> Psalm 137:1–6

9.
Merciful God, it amazes us that you do not deal with us as we deserve. We run from you, yet you stand ready to embrace us. We squander your gifts, yet you never cease bestowing your gifts upon us. There is nothing we can do to work ourselves back into your good graces, for in your eyes we were always your children and heirs of your grace. God, we don't understand how you can welcome us home, or why, but we accept your acceptance with eternal gratitude. Amen.

> 4th Lent, Year C
> Luke 15:1–3, 11–32

Easter

10.
Jesus our Savior, you call us to the narrow gate. Your way is difficult; the path lies uphill. But the door to your dwelling place is open—all who enter will be sustained and strengthened. By your

mercy and providence, lead us all to your threshold. Gird us with courage and hope that we may be pilgrims on your path now and forever. Amen.

4th Easter, Year A
John 10:1–10
(Matthew 7:13–14)

11.

Good Shepherd, the wolves are always among us, causing human pain and suffering. And we harbor wolf-selves that lash out to wound others. Deliver us and all people from our worst animal natures. With the gift of your transforming love, free us from the instinct to attack, and let it be our nature to love and shelter others. Amen.

4th Easter, Year B
John 10:11–18
1 John 3:18–24

12.

In your foolishness, O God,
You sent Jesus into our world as an infant
and wafted him out of our world with a cloud
While he walked the earth
words spilled from his mouth
that changed to bread in human hearts.
Wherever he roamed,
the sick and the lame followed;
the just and prosperous
walked away puzzled, fretting.
It was your doing, God,
to send a Savior like this.
We stumble headlong over his commands,
then find ourselves tripping
over what we have made of our lives.
You must have had a reason, God,
to order the world upside down.
Give us wisdom to understand the meaning
of all this foolishness. Amen.

Easter and Ascension
(Also 4th Epiphany, Year A)
(1 Corinthians 1:18–31)

Pentecost

13.
O God, you are compassionate, caring for the stubborn, feisty, and treacherous, as well as for the truthful, obedient, and loyal. We praise you that you are greater than our personalities, seeing what lies in our hearts, not judging us according to our public faces. Help us to see the Christ in others. Amen.

Pentecost, Year B
1 Samuel 16:1–13

14.
O Christ, all who call you Savior are pilgrims, following One who never stands still. Your Way leads us through rough and smooth terrain. Sometimes your path is seldom-used, overgrown, unpopular. Sometimes it is well-trodden. But always, as our way unfolds, we need the Light which only you can shed upon our path. When we are tempted to detour from your direction or to stagnate in dead ends, give us courage and renew our faith that the journey of our lives does indeed lead to the promised land of God's kingdom. Amen.

15.
Jesus our Christ, you know us in our promise and strength, as well as in our failure and weakness. By the grace of God you come to us, bidding us rise from our beds of affliction, helping us to claim your healing love. If the power of your words sways us and your mercy has grasped our hearts, grant that we may bring to others the affirmation and healing that we have found in you. Amen.

(John 5:2–9)

16.
Hidden and elusive God, things are not what they seem to be. Moses sees a bush afire; three visitors appear to Abraham and Sarah, leaving promises in their wake; a strong man wrestles with Jacob throughout the night. In all these disguises, you encountered your people. They wrestled with and entertained angels unaware. Even Christ our Savior was unrecognized on the Emmaus road, was mistaken as a ghost and as a gardener by those who loved him most. God of mystery, if you appear in the guise of stranger, then teach us with what care and kindness we should

treat each person we encounter. Grant that we may not turn you away, unaware of your many disguises. Amen.

3rd Pentecost, Year A
Genesis 32:22–32
(Exodus 3:1–6)
(Genesis 18:1–15)
(Hebrews 13:2)

17.
O God, the provisions you give for our journey have always been simple: something to eat, a path to follow, and a star to aim for. What you ask of us is equally simple: trust in you, trust in each other. The covenant between us is as simply beautiful as a rainbow spanning the sky; it is rough and sparse like the wood beams forming the cross. Wherever we go, whatever we do, remind us, God, of life's necessities: your great love for us, our love for you, and the opportunity to cherish each other. Amen.

7th Pentecost, Year B
Mark 6:7–13

18.
A Prayer of Sarah
O God, when your promises and our hopes are agonizingly slow to be fulfilled, teach us patient trust. When we feel impelled to help you move events more swiftly to our advantage, renew our faith and restrain us from headstrong acts. Teach us that delay of your promise doesn't mean that you have forsaken us. When we bear frustration, prevent us from badgering those we love and from using whoever is near for our own purpose. Amen.

(Genesis 16; 21:9–21)

19.
Loving God, your message is not sent in secret code, but in the plainest and simplest of words. It is a love letter to us. Help us to treasure it always, to live in love, and always to expect further messages. Amen.

20.
Dear Lord, you not only thunder solemn declarations, but you also belly-laugh, and your guffaws ring in our ears with Jesus' wit. Deliver us from using humor to mock or ridicule; help us to use

it with compassion. When we take ourselves too seriously, inject some levity into our situation. Deliver us from banana peels under our feet and cream pies in our face; but when we encounter them, grant us the grace to laugh at ourselves. Above all, help us to appreciate the punch line of your surprising grace and love. Amen.

21.
Without you, O God, we would be like frail boats drifting on a wild sea—anchorless, without direction, buffeted by every wind, and in peril of sinking. But we are not abandoned, O God. In Jesus Christ, you are close to shelter us and to save us. Your power anchors us against all storms. The light of your presence points the direction of our journey. We thank you, God, for your saving presence and the shelter of Jesus' love. Amen.

22.
O Gentle Shepherd, if we like sheep have gone astray, you eagerly seek us out, that not one may be lost. We thank you for such persistent and amazing love, which cares even for us. Amen.

18th Pentecost, Year C
Luke 15:1–10
(Isaiah 53:6)

23.
O God, lest we ever forget your promise of peace and shelter, anchor our hearts upon the unshakable foundation of your grace. In times of hesitation, doubt, or fear, remind us that at heart we are always your children, as you are always our God. And if we ever lose sight of this, you will never lose touch with us. Amen.

24.
In the heat of the day as in the cool of the night, O God, you call us and walk with us, as in the Garden of Eden. Help us not to hide, as did Adam and Eve, but give us courage to meet you, to listen attentively for your Word, and to labor with undaunted vision and patient love that all the earth may one day more closely resemble that first paradise. Amen.

20th Pentecost, Year B
Genesis 3:8–19

25.
God of strength, like Samson we casually tackle phenomenal feats as a matter of course. Taking the gifts you have given us for

granted, we may, without realizing it, squander and waste them as Samson did his physical gifts. Help us to use the gifts you have given with gratitude and responsibility lest, like Samson, we find that our greatest gift becomes our undoing. Amen.

(Judges 16)

26.
Compelling Spirit, we praise you for persistent love that out-maneuvers our inclination to evil. As you led Balaam, at last, to bless and not to curse, lead us also to serve you faithfully. May we disregard all temptation to destructive acts. And if we prove as imperceptive as Balaam, send us your naysaying angel to help us pause and consider whether the road we journey is indeed the path to your presence. Amen.

(Numbers 22)

PRAYERS OF DEDICATION

Epiphany

1.
As Jesus offered water changed to wine that his friends might rejoice, we offer these gifts, O God. With your grace may they be transformed into food and water, justice and peace. We give them that the world may rejoice in your work and presence. Amen.

2nd Epiphany, Year C
John 2:1–11

Lent

2.
O God, we bring these gifts in service of Christ, King of love and peace. Continue to shape us in the likeness of Christ who came not to be served, but to serve. Give us the strength to acclaim him even as he draws near to Jerusalem and the darkest night of trial. Amen.

Palm Sunday, Year C
Luke 19:28–40
(Matthew 20:28)

Easter

3.

LEADER: Christ is risen! He goes before us to Galilee. There we shall see him:

PEOPLE: As he moves among all the people, bringing promise to the poor, healing the troubled, and challenging the complacent.

LEADER: Now as in ancient Galilee, Christ works among us Now as then, he calls, "Follow me."

PEOPLE: O Risen Lord, the joy of your presence compels us to respond.

LEADER: Use these gifts to comfort and to heal, to strengthen and empower your people.

PEOPLE: Help us each day to trust your living presence and to serve all creation with Christlike compassion.

ALL: Amen.

Easter, Year B
Mark 16:1–15

4.

O God, we have heard your call, beckoning us to a life of love and service. Here, in daily, persistent, and sometimes courageous ways, we offer our lives for your service. We ask your blessing upon us and your continued grace to direct our path. Amen.

Pentecost

5.

LEADER: O God, our Savior has called for laborers to gather in the harvest.

PEOPLE: As you have given us rest and refreshment in your presence, we feel strengthened to answer his call.

LEADER: Privileged to be called co-workers of Christ,

PEOPLE: We offer all that we are and all that we do to be channels bringing his love and power into the world. Amen.

Pentecost, Year A
Matthew 9:35–10:8

6.

Yoked with you, O Jesus, there is no wisdom we cannot learn, no burden we cannot shoulder. We find wisdom, rest, and strength in your nearness. Thus we come to you, bearing our gifts for your service, and with fresh devotion we would love as you have loved us. Amen.

4th Pentecost, Year A
Matthew 11:25–30

7.
O Christ, you call out laborers for the harvest, and many hear your call. We praise you for accepting all kinds of people: bustling and forward like Martha; retiring and prayerful like Mary; impulsive and confident like Peter. Accept us also as those dedicated to your service and bless us this day. Amen.

8th Pentecost, Year C
Luke 10:1–12, 17–20

8.
LEADER: From the hand of God we receive ample provisions.
PEOPLE: Jesus, the Bread of Life, quells our hunger. Christ, the True Vine, quenches our thirst.
LEADER: If we are made one with him in love, let us live as he lives—
PEOPLE: With compassion that does not spurn the sick or the poor;
LEADER: With the generosity that gives out of poverty;
PEOPLE: With the humbleness to count self last and others with honor.
LEADER: Thus we offer ourselves to you, O Lord:
ALL: In gratitude for your gifts and the willingness to be poured out for others. Amen.

16th Pentecost, Year C
Luke 14:1, 7–14
(Mark 12:41–44)

9.
O Lord our God, in holiness and splendor and love so strong that the stars tremble, you have come to earth in Jesus Christ to love us and save us. In gratitude for the precious gift of life, we resolve this hour to love Christ with fresh devotion, to serve him with renewed energy, and to seek him in deepened prayer. O God, bless this our promise, that we may bear the fruit of Jesus' love into all the world. Amen.

CHARGES AND BLESSINGS

Advent and Christmas

1.
Rest in the assurance and comfort
that God shepherds you in wisdom,
gathers you to his side and holds you close,
never to release you to harm.
This is the season of mercy and of joy!
Go now in the strength of God's saving love
to shepherd the lone and the lost,
whom Christ would draw to his flock. Amen.

> 2nd Advent, Year B
> Isaiah 40:11
> (John 10:29; 21:15–17)

2.
Behold, the Lord proclaims to all the earth: "Your salvation has come!" You are God's holy people, the redeemed of the Lord, those he has sought out, never to be forsaken. As God delights and rejoices over you, go in peace, rejoicing in the Lord. Amen.

> Christmas
> Isaiah 62:(4–5) 11–12

Epiphany

3.
Go into the world doing what the Lord requires: living with kindness and justice, walking your path humbly, with God. Then you will find yourselves blessed.

Know that yours is the kingdom of heaven, yours the strength and mercy of God, yours all the blessings given to God's beloved children. Amen.

> 4th Epiphany, Year A
> Micah 6:8
> Matthew 5:1–12

4.
Follow Jesus wherever he goes—upon the mountain for prayer, into the valley to heal and to serve. Following the Savior requires of you both devotion and labor.

May the Spirit, the Counselor, provide wisdom and guidance for your journey. May the Spirit, the Comforter, give you empowering love. May the Spirit of truth summon you to labor with Christ for the redemption of the world. Amen.

> Transfiguration, Year C
> Luke 9:28–36
> (John 14:16–17)

Pentecost

5.
You are God's servants gifted with dreams and vision. Upon you rests the grace of God like flames of fire. Love and serve the Lord in the strength of the Spirit. May the deep peace of Christ be with you, the strong arms of God sustain you, and the power of the Holy Spirit strengthen you in every way. Amen.

> Day of Pentecost A,B,C
> Acts 2:1–21

6.
You are heirs according to the promise, children of the God of mercy. Therefore let your word be a resounding "yes!" Let hope prevail over despair. "The promise is to you and to your children, and to all that are far off, everyone whom God calls: Lo, I am with you always." Go in peace. Amen.

> Trinity Sunday, Year A
> Matthew 28:20
> (Galatians 3:29)
> (Acts 2:39)

7.
The God of all grace, who calls you to the eternal glory in Christ, restores, establishes, and strengthens you. Go now, refreshed by the Holy Spirit, strengthened in all wisdom and love, and established as God's child and disciple. Amen.

> (1 Peter 5:10, adapted)

8.
Be strong and of good courage; do not fear; for it is God who goes with you, and God will never fail nor forsake you. Go in peace. Amen.

> (Deuteronomy 31:6, adapted)

9.

Each of us has been given a gift, a portion of Christ's bounty. As each has received a gift, let us employ it for one another, as good stewards of God's varied grace.

Now may you walk in the light with the love of Christ, guided by the generous grace of God and the silent presence of the Holy Spirit, with you now and forever. Amen.

(Ephesians 4:7)
(1 Peter 4:10, adapted)

10.

Christ is your shepherd,
and in his presence
all your deepest needs are met,
your joy restored.
Into the chalice of your life
he pours mercy until it overflows.
Go now in peace, knowing
that all the days of your life
you dwell in the presence of the Lord. Amen.

(Psalm 23, adapted)

INDEX OF SCRIPTURAL REFERENCES

The number in each instance refers to the page on which the Scripture reference is given, even when the prayer begins on the preceding page.

INDEX OF DAYS
AND SEASONS

The number in each instance refers to the page on which the seasonal designation is given, even when the prayer begins on the preceding page.